Becoming the BEST Me

Third Edition

10 Career and Character Education Essentials

Bob Orndorff

jist Works
America's Career Publisher®

Becoming the Best Me, Third Edition
10 Career and Character Education Essentials

© 2009 by Robert Orndorff

Published by JIST Works, an imprint of JIST Publishing
7321 Shadeland Station, Suite 200
Indianapolis, IN 46256-3923

Phone: 800-648-JIST   Fax: 877-454-7839
E-mail: info@jist.com   Web site: www.jist.com

A Note to Instructors

An instructor's CD-ROM is available for this book (ISBN 978-1-59357-656-1). The instructor's CD-ROM includes ideas for discussion, additional exercises, classroom presentation slides, advice on how to fit character education into school programs, and solutions to workbook exercises.

Visit our Web site at www.jist.com. Find out about our products, order a catalog, and link to other career-related sites.

Quantity discounts are available for JIST books. Please call 800-648-JIST or visit www.jist.com for a free catalog and more information.

Trade and Workbook Product Manager: Lori Cates Hand
Contributing Editor: Dave Anderson
Cover and Interior Designer: Toi Davis
Proofreader: Jovana Shirley
Indexer: Jeanne Clark

15 14 13 12 11 10 09   9 8 7 6 5 4 3 2 1

ISBN 978-1-59357-655-4

Acknowledgments

With the many challenges taking place in our world today, I was committed to doing my part in providing at least a glimmer of hope and inspiration to our most precious American resource: our youth. This book, *Becoming the Best Me,* Third Edition, is therefore dedicated to my daughters Jessie and Addie, and to my son Zach, who give their mom and me a ton of joy and pride each and every day! Thank you kids for making my #1 goal in life crystal clear: Becoming the Best DAD! But the book is also dedicated to their cousins: Rocky, Julie, Bo, Olivia, Brooke, Andrew, Matthew, Ryann, Bennett, Brooke, David, Nathan, Derek, Dana, Isaac, Tanner, Brayden, Devin, Hannah, Connor, Shane, Kaitlin, Emily, Kim; to their friends: Cassidy, Ryan, Tyler, Carlee, Jake, Kyle, Alison, Michael, Nathan, Caleb, Reaney, Thomas, Samuel, Emily, Hannah, Becky, Jordan, Madison, Riley, Kara, Lauren; and to every child—not only in America, but as our kids say it, "in the whole wide world!"

Thank you to my cousins Art and Dave, brother-in-law Pete, and friend Keith for serving our country and fighting for a better world for our kids. I also want to thank the 11 organizations that offered quotes in this book: Accenture; Enterprise Rent-A-Car; IBM; Jefferson Pilot; Microsoft; Peace Corps; Pfizer; PricewaterhouseCoopers; Smart and Associates; United States Army; and Verizon. In addition to the companies, college students/graduates also contributed quotes and advice to students in this book, so a big thanks to the following Penn State students and recent graduates: Ellery Loomis, Jennifer Watkavitch, Michelle Ford, Michelle Kelly, Kristi Geist, Kim Brown, and Brian Jacobs. Finally, Mark Gustafson, the former President of Student Government at Elon University, shared his leadership experience and offered his advice within the Leadership chapter. Thanks, Mark!

A big thanks to the folks at JIST Publishing for their ongoing support and collegiality. In particular, I want to thank Lori Cates Hand, Product Line Manager; Selena Dehne, Publicist; and Barry Newborn, VP of Sales. JIST is made up of extremely talented people with tons of character and integrity.

As always, the people I owe the most gratitude are my family members, for writing this book was truly a family effort. Thanks first to my wife, Chris (Special Education certified), who always is willing to hear an earful, to proof my chapters, and to offer her professional opinion. Thanks to my sister Kelly, a high school math teacher, for contributing content to the book. Thanks to my dad, Bob, for coming up with the book's original title. A special thanks to my mom, Mary Lou, a recently retired middle school English teacher, who served as the editor-in-chief of the first edition. An extra-special thanks to my brother Erik, a middle-school teacher, for agreeing to write the Instructor's Manual for the second and third editions. Erik's ideas and activities help bring the featured 10 Career and Character Essentials to life—especially in the classroom!

About
Becoming the Best Me

Becoming the Best Me features 10 Career and Character Education Essentials that will help you succeed in school, at work, and in life. These essentials are highly sought after by company and college recruiters and include qualities such as diversity, communication, leadership, conflict resolution, teamwork, and community service.

Becoming the Best Me includes in-depth descriptions and real-life examples of the 10 essentials. Each chapter is devoted to a particular essential and contains strategies for developing that essential. You will also find direct quotes and advice from top company recruiters and successful college students throughout the book.

Developing these 10 essentials and incorporating them into your life can help you become the best you!

Contents

Before You Begin

One of the most important questions you'll need to answer in life is, "What do I want to be when I grow up?" You should continually explore careers and begin identifying those in which you're interested. **But what's even more important to answer right now in your life is, "What do I need to do in order to be successful in work AND in life?"** If you think about it, what does it really matter what career you choose if you're not going to be successful? And the reason you need to focus on this question NOW is that becoming successful doesn't happen when you're all grown up and out in the workforce; becoming successful is a process that starts early in your life and continues forever.

Simply put, nobody becomes great in a day. Do golfers hit par the first day they go golfing? Do artists paint their masterpieces the first time they pick up a brush? No! The best golfers and artists develop and sharpen their skills over a long period of time. It's common to hear a great golfer say, "I swung my first golf club before I could talk," or to hear a talented artist say, "I've been drawing for as long as I can remember."

Likewise, to *become the best you* in life, you have to start now. In this book, thousands of company recruiters nationwide indicate 10 essentials that make people successful in their career (see the surveys in Appendixes A, B, C, and D). All 10 are things that you should be developing now in order to be successful in life and in any career you choose. We call these "things" Career and Character Education Essentials, for these 10 essentials which are sought after by recruiters are the same 10 attributes found in the most successful people, in both work and in life. Behind every great worker is a great person of high character!

As you begin reading about the 10 Career and Character Education Essentials, take special note of the underlying qualities of each essential and the strategies presented to help you acquire each. After you clearly understand the 10 essentials and their strategies, start thinking of ways for *you* to begin developing all of these underlying qualities and ultimately take ownership of the 10 essentials.

Also take special note of all the direct quotes (presented throughout each chapter) that are offered by recruiters from 11 of the best organizations in America:

- **Accenture** (consulting firm)
- **Enterprise** (car rental company)
- **IBM** (technology firm)
- **Jefferson Pilot** (insurance and finance company)
- **Microsoft** (software company)
- **Peace Corps** (volunteer service organization)
- **Pfizer** (pharmaceutical company)
- **PricewaterhouseCoopers** (accounting firm)
- **Smart and Associates, LLP** (consulting firm)
- **U.S. Army** (federal government organization)
- **Verizon** (telecommunications company)

These top recruiters explain how the 10 Career and Character Education Essentials are valued and utilized within their respective companies. It's always good to get advice "straight from the horse's mouth!"

In addition to the recruiter quotes, you will also receive advice from current college students and recent graduates, primarily from Penn State University and Elon University. These college students offer their views on the importance of the 10 Career and Character Education Essentials and share experiences they had in high school that helped them become successful in college.

As you develop the 10 essentials, you should strongly consider tracking these essential experiences and attributes in an electronic portfolio, better known as an *e-portfolio* (see Appendix E). We're in a "just do it and move on" society, racing from one experience to the next without taking time to reflect on what we learned and what skills we developed. Developing and maintaining an e-portfolio will enable you to take stock of your skills and accomplishments and successfully market yourself to college and company recruiters. Appendix E presents the ins and outs of developing your very own e-portfolio!

Finally, I hope you enjoy learning about the 10 Career and Character Education Essentials and making them a part of you. I've included many examples and stories that I think you'll relate to which will help bring key points to life and add a little entertainment value. It can actually be a lot of fun working toward *becoming the best you!*

Career and Character Education Essential #1

Become a People Person

"Strong interpersonal skills are the cornerstone for being considered for almost every job at Microsoft. This starts in the interview process as soon as a candidate is contacted. If the candidate cannot interact effectively with recruiters, how will that person be effective in communicating with his/her manager, other employees, and—most importantly— the customer?"

—Microsoft

What Is a "People Person?"

A *people person* is another (more informal) way to describe someone who has strong *interpersonal* skills. And a person with strong interpersonal skills is someone who is able to relate well with a wide variety of people and who loves to be with people.

What Is the Difference Between Interpersonal and Communication Skills?

Before we jump right in and start talking about the ins and outs of interpersonal skills, let's make sure we know what we mean when we say someone has strong interpersonal skills. A lot of people refer to *interpersonal* and *communication* skills interchangeably. After listening to a speaker, a member in the audience may say to her friend, "Boy, she really has strong interpersonal skills." Or, if someone gets along well with others, people tend to say, "He really communicates well with people."

"Interpersonal skills come into play in a variety of ways, every day at Microsoft. Software design engineers must be able to interact effectively with their colleagues to complete projects; product managers must be able to communicate with senior management about product strategy; and senior management needs to be able to sell their ideas for developing, marketing, and selling products to their fellow senior leaders, including Steve Ballmer and Bill Gates."

—Microsoft

So are they one and the same? If people are able to communicate well, do they naturally have strong interpersonal skills? Let's take a look at the following exchange between two high school friends, Addie and Olivia.

Olivia: Addie, tell me what you think about the opening paragraph of my research paper. I put a lot of time into it; I need the opening to be strong.

Addie: The first sentence is written very poorly. The incorporation of adjectives used to describe the author leaves much to be desired. I would seriously consider starting over.

Olivia: Just forget it! Sorry I bothered you!

Did Addie verbally communicate her thoughts well? Communicating well means that you're able to articulate your thoughts clearly and fluently. Was it clear what Addie was trying to tell Olivia? I'd say it was crystal clear. Addie's communication skills were strong. How were her interpersonal skills? Having strong interpersonal skills has to do with how well you relate to others and how well your expressed thoughts and actions are received. A big part of being interpersonal is having a level of sensitivity to others and expressing yourself tactfully.

Was Addie very tactful when giving feedback to Olivia? Not really. Was she sensitive to the fact that Olivia put a lot of time in writing this opening paragraph? No, she wasn't. So, in this scenario, it is pretty safe to say that Addie demonstrated strong communication skills and weak interpersonal skills. Take a look at a different exchange that occurred between Addie and Olivia.

Student Quote

"Being a people person is something that is essential to any career, no matter what field a student pursues. Becoming involved on an extracurricular level early on in high school will only give students more of an opportunity to refine their communication skills as they continue throughout their educational journey. A confident communicator translates into confidence in demeanor both in and out of the classroom and workplace."

—*Jennifer Watkavitch, recent graduate*

Olivia: Addie, tell me what you think about the opening paragraph of my research paper. I put a lot of time into it; I need the opening to be strong.

Addie: Well, like, the first sentence, was, like, good—don't get me wrong, but, um, it maybe could use a tad more enthusiasm. Um, also, like, I really liked overall how you, um, were, trying to like describe that author guy. But, um, I don't know, I think maybe we could think of a different word to describe him than, like, awesome.

Olivia: Thanks a lot, Addie. I'll get right on that!

How would you rate Addie this time around? How well did she communicate her thoughts? Was she articulate, clear, and fluent? No. Certainly, few people would say Addie possessed strong communication skills in this recent scenario. But how were her interpersonal skills? Was Addie a little more sensitive towards Olivia? Absolutely. Don't you think that Olivia would receive Addie's feedback less defensively this second time around? Therefore, during this second scenario, Addie demonstrated stronger interpersonal skills than she did before, but her communication skills were much weaker. So, it IS possible to have very strong communication skills and very poor interpersonal skills, and vice versa.

As the preceding scenarios illustrated, tactfulness and sensitivity are basic interpersonal skills. But there is more to it. In the next part of this chapter, we're going to describe several qualities that enable someone to have strong interpersonal skills—in other words, to be a people person.

Identifying and Developing the Qualities of a People Person

It's not enough for you to say, "I want to become a people person," or "I want to develop my interpersonal skills." Just how would you develop your interpersonal skills? Beneath strong interpersonal skills are a number of personal qualities. The trick is to understand what these qualities are, and then work on making them a part of you. The following are descriptions of six key qualities of a people person, as well as some pointers on how you can develop these qualities. Acquiring these strong qualities is very important to the development of strong interpersonal skills.

1. Awareness/Conscientiousness

Remember that a fundamental aspect of being a people person is *being able to relate well with others.* In order to relate well with others, you must be aware of other people and their feelings. Some people refer to this quality as having "street sense." Someone who has good street sense has a good feel or understanding of his or her surroundings. You can sense what is going on and therefore anticipate others' actions. For example, if you have good street sense, you will be able to anticipate a fight or sense a bad situation coming on. You will know when someone is down and take action to help that person feel better. Being conscientious is thinking through and caring about the consequences of your actions. Thus, in order to relate well with others, you must always be aware of people's states of mind and feelings, and be conscientious (careful) in what you say and how you act around them.

> ## Student Quote
>
> "Interpersonal skills are very important, especially after you get into college. It is crucial to be able to communicate with students in your classes as well as your professors in order to do well in any given course. I developed my interpersonal skills by joining Key Club, which is a community service club. I was able to help people and work with fellow students. Another way to develop interpersonal skills would be to run for office in student government, a club at school, or a religious affiliated group. Being an officer in a club forces you to work with people even more than just being a member."
>
> —*Michelle Kelly, education major*

2. Diplomacy/Tactfulness

"Strong interpersonal skills and the ability to adapt in conversation will allow individuals to remain resilient in the following situations: conversing with ease, negotiating, handling criticism, coaching someone to improve performance, and expressing dissatisfaction effectively."

—Verizon

Being diplomatic or tactful goes hand in hand with being aware and conscientious. This quality, however, focuses more on your actions than on your thoughts or gut instincts. Being aware of the feelings of others enables you to act diplomatically or tactfully. Let's examine a couple of scenarios to better understand diplomacy and tact:

Zach and Andrew are members of the Politics Club at their school. Various club members are engaged in a debate about raising taxes. Andrew believes in raising taxes, and Zach is against it. After Andrew gives his argument for raising taxes, Zach replies:

"Obviously, Andrew has no idea what he's talking about. Hey, Andrew, when you make an argument, it helps to actually know something about the subject. People who think that raising taxes is the answer don't have a clue!"

Behaving tactfully means that you will choose your words wisely so that you do not offend or embarrass someone. Was Zach diplomatic or tactful in this situation? Not at all. And would you say that this lack of diplomacy will hurt his chances of relating well with Andrew and others who are on Andrew's side? Let's look at a more tactful Zach.

"I understand where Andrew is coming from. His point on raising taxes for the benefit of children makes some sense. However, I believe that there is a broader issue that we should be considering."

You see, being tactful doesn't mean that you have no backbone and that you have to agree with everyone all the time. You *can disagree* with others and stand up for what you believe in *without offending* others. It is all in how you package your argument. Don't be afraid to disagree or confront someone, just do it tactfully. And remember, sometimes doing it tactfully means that you have to calm yourself down before you respond to someone. It's hard being tactful when your emotions get the best of you. Take a deep breath or two, be aware of who you're talking to, think about what you'd like to say, and go for it. You will learn much more about dealing with conflicts and confronting others in Chapters 3 and 4.

"Any interaction with a client requires solid interpersonal skills. Whether in a presentation, negotiation, or discussion, Accenture personnel build rapport by engaging others in a congenial and professional way."

—Accenture

3. Ability to Actively Listen

"Interpersonal skills are critical in team environments. In a dynamically changing corporate environment, employees must remain strong and rely on the power of strong communication, which includes communication through listening as well as through dialogue."

—Verizon

One of the most underrated personal qualities is being a good listener. Stop and think for a minute about the people that you know who are good listeners. Don't you love them? In this hustle and bustle world, it's a treat to have someone who really listens to you. What a gift to give to others when you're able to put all the stuff that is going on in your life aside and actively listen to them! There is simply no better interpersonal quality to have than to give of yourself and really be there for someone who needs it. You may think that you are fooling people into thinking that you're listening, but most people can tell when you're not. Here's an example of a poor listener.

Student Quote

"In high school you gain most of your interpersonal skills through socializing with your friends, but to truly gain the interpersonal skills necessary for success you must go out of your comfort zone and try to socialize with people that you know nothing about. This way you not only are meeting new people, but you are also meeting people that surprisingly share a common interest with you."

—Kim Brown, recent graduate

> **Dave:** Hey Art, how's it going?
>
> **Art:** Not so good.
>
> **Dave:** Cool.
>
> **Art:** Hey Dave, you got a minute?
>
> **Dave:** Sure.
>
> **Art:** Man, I might have blown my chances of getting into college. I think I may get a "C" in pre-calculus.
>
> **Dave:** Ah, don't let it bother you. Hey, are you going to the concert on Friday? How did you get your ticket?

Was Dave *actively* listening to Art? Was he able to put his issues aside and really be there for Art? Dave started off by asking how Art was doing, and he responded, "Cool," when Art said, "Not so good." Is Dave someone you would call a people person? A people person is someone you like to be around. It's not much fun being around someone who doesn't listen to you. Let's give Dave another shot. The following is an example of "Active Listening Dave."

> **Dave:** Hey Art, how's it going?
>
> **Art:** Not so good.
>
> **Dave:** Really? What's up?
>
> **Art:** Man, I might have blown my chances of getting into college. I think I may get a "C" in pre-calculus.
>
> **Dave:** Are you serious? Darn it. Why do you think you may get a "C"?

Now Dave is being an active listener. One of the best ways to show that you are listening actively to someone is by asking follow-up questions. None of us wants to bore people with our problems, but when people give you the green light by asking follow-up questions, it sure is nice! This may all seem elementary, but when you have a thousand things on your mind as most people do, it's difficult to be unselfish and actively listen.

The best way to become more of an active listener (if you're not already) is to be aware of your natural tendency to drift off or lose focus when people are talking to you. When you start to consciously catch yourself not really listening, you can begin to change this habit by learning to put your concerns away for a while and listen. You will be surprised how good you feel about yourself when you do this.

"Our consultants conduct information-gathering interviews with our clients' employees to understand the 'as-is' state of a particular business process. At times, our client's employees may feel anxious about sharing information (talking and listening) with outsiders. It is critical that our consultants use their strong interpersonal skills to gain the trust of these employees so that they can gather the information needed for the analysis."

—PricewaterhouseCoopers

4. Open-Mindedness

Once again, being able to relate well with others is at the essence of interpersonal skills. However, what's key in an increasingly diverse world and workforce is relating well with a wide variety of people from diverse cultures and backgrounds. The only way to do this is to be open-minded. You have learned by now that not everyone looks like you, thinks like you, acts like you, or believes everything you believe. A key to being open-minded and ultimately *becoming the best you* is accepting the fact that there is not one right way of doing things or one right way of being. Open-minded people are intrigued by differences in others rather than frustrated that others are not more like them. You don't have to like everyone, but you should always respect their differences. In the next chapter, we will go into much greater depth about being open to differences and truly appreciating diversity. For now, just remember that it is an oxymoron to say that someone who does not appreciate diversity is a people person!

5. Humility (Humble)

People naturally like others who are humble. Very few people like those who brag about themselves. Think how you feel about someone who boastfully tells you he got an "A" on a paper versus someone who didn't tell you

Student Quote

"Many times, your interpersonal skills are the mark by which people judge you. If you are applying for a job, internship, college, or even any extracurricular activity, your interpersonal and communication skills might be what separates you from everyone else. In the end, people will judge you not by your GPA, but by your ability to express yourself and communicate and work well with others."

—Brian Jacobs,
political science major

he got an "A" until you asked him, and then tells you he got lucky. Don't you feel better about yourself when you keep your successes to yourself, and only reveal them when people ask or take note?

Part of being humble is being unselfish. Can you think of people you know who always are talking about themselves?

> "Hey, guess what happened to me?"
>
> "You guys, I am so happy. I aced the test today."
>
> "You should have seen me last night. I played better than I ever have."

When you are at a party or just hanging out with friends, the unselfish thing to do is to ask others how they are doing.

> "Hey, Julie, how's your day been?"
>
> "What's up, Bo? How'd you do on that test you were studying for?"
>
> "Rocky, how'd you do last night? Did you win your match?"

A selfish person will always initiate things about himself or herself. A people person will ask others about their lives.

6. Good Sense of Humor

> "Interpersonal skills are another way to describe being able to sell yourself. Whether you're with a client or working on a global project, you will need to have self-confidence, a positive attitude, maturity, a team orientation, fluency of expression (nonverbal many times being very important outside the U.S.), and humor."
>
> —IBM

How many times have you heard someone say, "I really like her; she's so funny." Or, "He has a good sense of humor; he's a great guy." People like others who have a sense of humor. It's fun to be around someone who makes you laugh. We live in a fast-paced, dog-eat-dog world. Isn't it nice to take a break occasionally and have a good laugh?

If you want to develop a good sense of humor, don't go out and buy a joke book and force jokes on everyone. The best way to develop your sense of humor is to relax, be yourself, and don't take everything so seriously. It's healthy to be able to laugh at yourself. You're not going to be perfect every day of your life. Everyone has a bloopers highlight video—but not everyone is secure enough to share it. Remember to keep things in perspective, lighten your stress load, and laugh occasionally.

How to Become More of a People Person

The first step in becoming a people person and developing strong interpersonal skills is to understand and value the six underlying personal qualities presented previously. The second step is to take an honest look at yourself and determine which of these qualities you already possess and which ones you need to develop. Ask people who know you best to give you honest feedback regarding how these qualities apply to you. This second step is very important. You know what they say: "Once you admit to something, you're halfway there!"

After this is done, it's time for you to get out there and mix it up with people. But this time, as you interact with others, try to incorporate as many of these qualities as you can. Whether you're in class, at practice, or just hanging out with your friends, try your best to be a positive people person! For example, when you're talking with someone, try extra-hard to actively listen to him or her. When you disagree with someone, state why you disagree in a tactful way. Look for the good things in people and compliment them on those things rather than pointing out the bad. Ask people about their day before telling them all about you and your day. In other words, take these interpersonal characteristics out on the road with you as you carry out your typical day.

Finally, make it a habit to analyze your various interactions with people at the end of each day. Reflect on the qualities that you carried out well and those which you struggled with. Think about what you could have done differently to be more effective interpersonally. The more you reflect, the more you'll be able to develop those interpersonal qualities that need the most work. It's important

Student Quote

"Activities outside the classroom are important to meeting new people, releasing the tension of a heavy workload, and overall happiness and well-being. Going back to my dorm room or apartment after class instead of participating in something that I have interest in is conducive to nothing but boredom, procrastination, and mismanagement of time."

—Brian Jacobs, political science major

to realize that every single person has the potential of becoming a people person, but for some it takes more effort. It takes more than just learning about the six underlying qualities—you have to be committed to making them qualities of your own!

Why Company Recruiters Put Interpersonal Skills at the Top of Their Wish Lists

"It is important that our company hires graduates that possess strong interpersonal skills, because doing the specific job is only part of the overall skill of doing the entire job. Being able to relate with other individuals is more than 50 percent of what's needed to be a great employee."

—Jefferson Pilot

With all the excitement centered on modern technology and the importance of having computer skills, you might think that computer skills would be on the top of recruiters' wish lists. Or due to the importance of solving new problems and life-long learning, wouldn't analytical skills be most important? It turns out that over the past 5 to 10 years, interpersonal skills have been on or near the top of the wish lists of most recruiters. Why?

When recruiters are asked, "Why are interpersonal skills more important than some of the other key skills?" most give an answer similar to the one below.

"When we need employees to learn a new computer application, we can train them on that. If employees need to brush up on their communication skills, there are plenty of communication seminars out there to send them to. However, if employees come to us without good interpersonal skills, it takes much more than trying to enhance a skill or two; it's trying to change the type of person that they are! For example, how do you train an insensitive person to become more sensitive when confronting others? How can we train someone to be more positive if he or she is naturally a more negative person? How do we get people who bring 20 years worth of stereotypes with them to appreciate diversity?"

Remember, good interpersonal skills incorporate a host of personal qualities that have been presented in this chapter. Training someone to have stronger interpersonal skills means that you have to change many personal qualities that make up that person.

Besides the difficulty of helping a person become a people person, there is another main reason interpersonal skills are so valued by recruiters: These skills greatly affect the chemistry and morale within companies. Someone's negative interpersonal skills can have a negative impact on many of the employees around him. Conversely, an employee who has strong interpersonal skills can have a positive influence on others and help make the work atmosphere more pleasant. Remember, interpersonal skills are contagious!

THE WHOLE IN ONE

- Interpersonal skills and communication skills are definitely not the same. You can have one without the other.
- There are six qualities that enable one to possess strong interpersonal skills:
  1. Awareness/conscientiousness
  2. Diplomacy/tactfulness
  3. Ability to actively listen
  4. Open-mindedness
  5. Humility (humble)
  6. Good sense of humor
- Recruiters place interpersonal skills at the top of their wish lists because they are much harder to develop, and because they have a big impact on the morale of a team.

BECOME THE BEST YOU . . . BECOME A PEOPLE PERSON!

Chapter 1 Review

Read each question and circle the *best* answer.

1. **A person with great communication skills**

    a. has great interpersonal skills.

    b. has terrible interpersonal skills.

    c. doesn't necessarily have great interpersonal skills.

    d. is sensitive to others' feelings.

2. **When someone has great interpersonal skills, she/he is one who**

    a. speaks well in front of a group.

    b. tells people what to do.

    c. leads by example.

    d. relates well and is received positively by people.

3. **When Addie told Olivia that the first sentence was written very poorly, Addie lacked**

    a. communication skills.

    b. honesty.

    c. tact and sensitivity.

    d. humor.

4. **To be a great people person, you need to be aware of people's**

    a. feelings.

    b. strengths.

    c. beliefs.

    d. weaknesses.

5. **Diplomacy and tactfulness focus more on your**

    a. attitude.

    b. actions.

    c. gut instincts.

    d. awareness.

(continued)

(continued)

6. **The best way to improve your active listening skills is to be aware of your**
   a. surroundings.
   b. eye contact.
   c. posture.
   d. tendency to lose focus.

7. **Being able to laugh at yourself depends on your level of**
   a. security.
   b. humor.
   c. charisma.
   d. "spunk."

8. **The most effective way to show that you are listening is to**
   a. use eye contact.
   b. sit up straight.
   c. nod your head in agreement.
   d. ask follow-up questions.

9. **Jefferson Pilot states that _____ are more than half of what is needed to be a great employee.**
   a. listening skills
   b. computer skills
   c. interpersonal skills
   d. communication skills

10. **According to Chapter 1, good interpersonal skills are**
    a. fun.
    b. contagious.
    c. awesome.
    d. spectacular.

2

Career and Character Education Essential #2

Appreciate Diversity

"When you look at the country and the changing face of the population, it becomes clear that having a diverse workforce and supplier network is not just a good idea, but an essential one. It is a goal at Enterprise to have our workforce mirror the communities in which we do business, and all of our employees need to understand the importance of having a company that supports and respects all people. In short, we strive to ensure that our company is inclusive and supportive of people of all backgrounds."

—Enterprise Rent-A-Car

Defining the Phrase "Appreciate Diversity"

A person who really appreciates diversity realizes the many benefits it brings to a team, group, or community. It's important, however, to clarify what we mean when we say "appreciate diversity." First of all, what do we mean by "diversity?" *Diversity* is another way of saying *differences* or *variations*. Most of us think of racial differences when we hear the term diversity. However, there are many other types of diversity. Below are some examples of types of diversity found in the workplace and in life:

- *Ethnic/racial:* African-American, Asian-American, Hispanic-American, Native American, etc.
- *Gender:* female, male
- *Disability status:* visually impaired, hearing impaired, paralyzed, etc.
- *Citizenship:* U.S. citizen, foreign national, international student, etc.
- *Sexual orientation:* heterosexual, homosexual, bisexual, etc.
- *Religious affiliation:* Catholic, Jewish, Muslim, Protestant, etc.
- *Marital and family status:* married, single, divorced, single parent, etc.
- *Socioeconomic status:* wealthy, poor, unemployed, on welfare, homeless, etc.
- *Geographic/regional:* southerners, New Englanders, etc.
- *Height and weight:* tall, short, skinny, overweight, etc.
- *Hair color:* blond, auburn, brunette, etc.
- *Personality:* funny, shy, outgoing, etc.
- *Intelligence:* smart, stupid, nerdy, etc.
- *Work ethic:* lazy, hardworking, etc.

Student Quote

"When I was in high school, you could walk down the hallway and see one group standing by the lockers speaking Spanish, another group speaking Chinese, and of course, a larger whole speaking English. This would be a great thing except for one problem—they were still groups that stayed within their own cultural boundaries. It is great to be exposed to a diverse range of people and cultures; however, is it true diversity if everyone sticks to their own groups?"

—Brian Jacobs,
political science major

"It is important for us to hire people that possess an appreciation of diversity because people of different backgrounds—socially, economically, and ethnically—are people that provide a pool of creative ideas and resources that the entire team can draw from."

—Jefferson Pilot

This list, while not all-inclusive, should give you an idea of how many different types of diversity there are. It's important that you broaden your concept of diversity and think about the many ways people are different from you and from one another.

"A good example of when an appreciation of diversity benefits Microsoft is how the company continues to develop products that have functionality for persons with disabilities. One out of five Americans (according to the National Organization on Disability), and therefore one out of five customers, has a disability. Through an appreciation for diversity, Microsoft recognizes that information technology is one of the most important enabling factors for persons with disabilities in the workplace."

—Microsoft

We also need to understand what the word *appreciate* means in the phrase "appreciate diversity." Looking at the difference between appreciating diversity and tolerating diversity can help us better understand what this is all about.

Appreciating Diversity vs. Tolerating Diversity

"Diversity at Accenture is a top priority because solutions to complex business problems are best solved by people with different backgrounds. Accenture fosters an environment rich in diversity that acknowledges each individual's uniqueness; values his or her skills and contributions; and promotes respect, personal achievement, and stewardship. 'Respect for the individual' is one of our core values, and we strive to build an inclusive environment in which all employees feel valued and appreciated."

—Accenture

Unfortunately, there are too many people in this world who only tolerate diversity. When someone tolerates diversity, they don't really believe in the benefits of diversity. They keep their real feelings and biases to themselves and go through the motions because they feel it's something they have to accept. Let me give you an example.

THE TOLERATING BANKER

Joe, a white male, works at a bank. Joe comes from a small, rural town, where there were hardly any racial minority members. In his town growing up, it was common to tell racist jokes and to put down people from different races and cultures. Thus, overall, Joe had developed a bias against racial minority people. However,

(continued)

(continued)

as part of the training program at his bank, Joe learned about the bank's philosophy of being open and appreciating people from all cultures and backgrounds. It was clear that an employee could be fired if this philosophy is not upheld. Recently, the bank hired an Asian-American teller, Greg. Joe was not happy about this, and he felt uncomfortable talking to Greg. One day, Greg asked Joe if he would make a photocopy for him. Joe didn't like taking orders from Greg, but he did it anyway. Joe resents Greg for asking him to do this and now tries to avoid him as much as possible.

I wish I could say this never happens anymore. However, this kind of passive racism still exists. Joe clearly does not appreciate Greg and the ways in which he can make positive contributions to the bank, but he is willing to keep his mouth shut so he doesn't get fired. In other words, Joe merely tolerates Greg in order to keep his job.

When you appreciate diversity, you respect the differences in others and appreciate the added value that these differences can bring. To become the best you, you must make a strong effort to learn how to appreciate diversity!

Student Quote

"I have had the opportunity to live and work with people from every walk of life. This has truly assisted me in everything that I have done. Knowing and respecting what makes people unique and what things are important to them can truly increase one's success in any career field."

—Ellery Loomis,
recent graduate

Learning to Appreciate Diversity

"Our current and future business is based on our ability to respect and embrace many different cultures. Our employees need to have the same appreciation for the benefits of embracing and working with people who come from many different backgrounds and bring different experiences to the table. Respecting diversity is the only way an organization can be successful long-term in the global economy."

—PricewaterhouseCoopers

Talking about diversity, especially regarding race, gender, and sexual orientation, is a sensitive subject for many people. The delicate nature of diversity keeps us from dealing with it more openly. However, with the workplace and our world becoming increasingly more diverse, it is imperative that you take the steps necessary to develop your appreciation of and belief in diversity. People need to take a good hard look at themselves regarding their thoughts and feelings about diversity issues.

Follow the Three-Step Plan

The following is a three-step plan to further develop your appreciation of diversity.

Step One: Own Up to Your Biases and Prejudices

People are embarrassed to admit that they have biases and prejudices toward certain groups of people. The term *prejudiced* is especially harsh for most people. To say that someone is prejudiced implies that that person is a bad person. Our natural instinct is to defend ourselves, so we deny having any biases or prejudices. And, because "we are not prejudiced," we don't have to deal with the issue, right?

> ## Student Quote
>
> "Even if you live in a place where there isn't much diversity in race, religion, and socioeconomic backgrounds, there are still ways to reach out and understand the importance of diversity. There are programs like Big Brother and Big Sister in which you can help a child, who may not live in the environment that you live in, get a better start in life."
>
> —Kim Brown,
> recent graduate

The first step that we all have to take is to stop thinking of prejudice and bias as a huge stigma, because if we continue to think of it in this way, we will continue to deny our biases and fail to do anything about them.

We all have biases—accept it and move on!

We were all born and raised in different towns and cities, some of which had a great deal of diversity, others that had very little. Parents, grandparents, sisters and brothers, uncles and aunts, cousins, friends, teachers, coaches, and many other people have influenced us all. We all are part of a certain ethnic and racial culture and have varying religious beliefs. Because of all of these influences and associations, there is no way that you could not have developed some emotional leanings toward a certain side. If you never had the opportunity to interact with certain groups of people, how could you possibly avoid having preconceived opinions about these groups of people?

It's time for people to stop beating themselves up for having biases and prejudices. Only then will you be able to more openly explore and challenge your biases. The thoughts and feelings that you have toward certain groups of people do exist. It's okay that you have them. However, it is *not* okay to deny them and to do nothing about them!

Step Two: Catch Yourself and Identify Your Biases and Prejudices

Admitting that you have biases is a big part of the battle. The next step is to be aware of the biases and prejudices that you have and learn to catch yourself when you have these thoughts and feelings. If you cannot identify your biases and prejudices, how can you ever explore and question them? Consider the following example.

> Pat, a high school student in Connecticut, is taking a marketing class. A big part of the class was to complete a semester-long team project. The teacher was pairing off students in teams of two. Pat was hoping to be teamed up with a good student who would carry his or her weight. The teacher assigned Jennifer to work with Pat. Jennifer's family recently moved from Georgia to Connecticut and she had a thick, southern accent. Because he was from the North, Pat had a bias in favor of northerners who he believed worked quickly and completed tasks efficiently and effectively. He stereotypes southerners as people who move at a slow pace and are a little flighty. Pat had a preconceived opinion of Jennifer.

Now, if Pat isn't acutely aware of this prejudice, he'll probably treat Jennifer with little respect and think that he has to do all the work to get an "A." However, if Pat is able to *catch himself* and admit that he is being biased, he may give Jennifer a chance.

Step Three: Challenge Your Biases and Give Everyone a Chance

As you catch yourself and identify your biases, you need to *challenge* the bias or prejudice that is staring you in the face and give the person with whom you are interacting a chance. Give all people the respect they deserve by treating them as unique human beings. The following is a story I once heard from an African-American speaker that emphasizes the importance of giving people a chance.

Student Quote

"Keep an open mind about every situation and every person you meet. By limiting your social circle to just those people who are in your classes and involved in your extracurricular activities, you could be missing out on exciting life experiences and life-long friends."

—Kristi Geist,
management major

"Last week I had a long flight across the country. As I got on the plane, I noticed that my seat was right next to this big country-looking guy! I mean, he was all dressed up like a cowboy, with his cowboy hat, cowboy shirt, tight pants, and cowboy boots. My first instinct was to think, 'Man, why me! Why do I have to sit next to this redneck for the whole trip? Well, I'm not gonna talk to this idiot!' But then, I caught myself! Even though he looked like a redneck, I challenged myself to be a big person and not write this guy off. So I started a conversation by introducing myself. Well, we weren't like best friends or anything, but we talked once in a while during this long trip, and he wasn't all that bad. And most importantly, I felt pretty good about going against my natural instinct to write him off! If each of you would just do that, the world would be a much better place!"

What a great message! When you start feeling negative toward certain people, don't just write them off; challenge that feeling (bias) and give them a chance! You should also remember that you *can* influence and control your feelings and emotions. Keeping an open mind and thinking positively can *feed* your heart in a healthy way.

AN OLD INDIAN GRANDFATHER

An old Indian grandfather said to his grandson who came to him
with anger at a friend who had done him an injustice...
"Let me tell you a story. I too, at times, have felt a great
hate for those that have taken so much, with no sorrow for what
they do. But hate wears you down, and does not hurt your enemy.
It is like taking poison and wishing your enemy would die.
I have struggled with these feelings many times."
He continued...
"It is as if there are two wolves inside me;
One is good and does no harm. He lives in harmony with all
around him and does not take offense when no offense was
intended. He will only fight when it is right to do so, and in
the right way. He saves all his energy for the right fight.
But the other wolf, ahhh!

(continued)

(continued)

He is full of anger. The littlest thing will set him into a
fit of temper. He fights everyone, all the time, for no reason.
He cannot think because his anger and hate are so great. It is
helpless anger, for his anger will change nothing.
Sometimes it is hard to live with these two wolves inside me,
for both of them try to dominate my spirit."
The boy looked intently into his grandfather's eyes and asked...
"Which one wins, Grandfather?"
The grandfather smiled and quietly said...
"The one I feed."

—Indian Author (Unknown)

We all need to feed the positive feelings and thoughts we have toward others rather than the petty negative ones.

Get Involved in Multicultural Experiences

Diversity is all around you. You have an opportunity every day to interact with people from different backgrounds, cultures, and orientations. Challenge yourself and get to know a wide variety of people. Also, make sure you take full advantage of the plethora of multicultural experiences that are available. The following are opportunities you might encounter that will help you to develop your appreciation for diversity.

Study a Foreign Language

"Volunteers live in communities overseas where English is not the primary language that is spoken. Thus, there is a need to learn a new language. In addition, not only does a volunteer need to learn a new language, they must be able to communicate with host country nationals to succeed in the goals of their projects."

—Peace Corps

Many countries require children to learn to speak more than one language. Unfortunately, the United States is not one of them. Even though lately there has been a greater push to learn how to speak Spanish, as a nation we don't emphasize the importance of being bilingual as much as we should. However, there are plenty of opportunities in school to learn how to speak a second language. Most schools offer courses on speaking, reading, and writing a foreign language. Use the wonderful resources that you have at your fingertips to learn a different language. There will be no other time in your life that you will have this convenient of an opportunity to do so. Take advantage of it now! Later, if you go to college, you can even major or minor in a foreign language and culture. French and Spanish are two traditional majors. Foreign language study opens doors to understanding and appreciating other cultures.

Take a Multicultural/Race-Relations Course

Many schools offer at least one course on diversity, usually called *Multicultural Issues*, *Race Relations*, or *Ethnic and Racial Diversity*. During the class, you will learn about different cultures and about people with different orientations and religious beliefs. You'll learn about the barriers that prevent people from getting along and the key factors of integration. You may even have a chance to engage in open dialogue with classmates that come from different races and backgrounds. You'll also learn a lot about yourself and your own biases and prejudices.

Study or Travel Abroad

Traveling to a different country is a wonderful way to develop your appreciation of diversity. You should also look into opportunities for studying abroad. Talk to your school counselor about the possibility of becoming an exchange student for a semester or year. Usually you will be able to choose from among several different countries. While you are there, make sure you soak in the culture and get to know the locals. Learn about the prevalent religion(s), customs, norms, and values. Spend as much time as you can with people from different cultures. It's tempting to just hang out with your family or, if studying abroad, with fellow students from your own country, but you'll be missing out on half of the learning experience if you don't get out there and meet different people. Remember to be aware of your biases and

Student Quote

"Diversity is of the utmost importance and something every student should value. I would suggest trying something outside of your comfort level such as going to a group activity or meeting that you normally wouldn't attend. Try something different and learn from it. Take those experiences and feelings and strive to incorporate diversity in your everyday life."

—*Michelle Ford, communication arts major*

to challenge your preconceived opinions as you meet people who are different from you.

As a career counselor and advisor, I have found that when students consider studying abroad, they are often apprehensive about leaving their homeland and living in a new country and culture. It's always fun to see the big smile on their faces when they return. The students always come back saying that it was the best experience of their lives, and that it has changed their perspectives on life. Don't miss out on this life-changing opportunity if you get the chance to study abroad!

Rent the Movie *Remember the Titans*

There are a number of movies and videos out there that center on racism and diversity. However, one of the more recent ones that should be seen by every high school student is *Remember the Titans*, starring Denzel Washington. This movie effectively delivers the message that when students from a different race are forced to spend quality time together, they eventually get to know and appreciate the person underneath the skin color.

You Can Make a Difference

You can make a difference. Your attitude and actions can have a profound effect upon those around you. There is no better example of this than the story of Rosa Parks. In Montgomery, Alabama, in December 1955, Parks boarded a bus after a long day of work. She was tired, and so she took an open seat. The bus grew more crowded and Parks, an African-American woman, was ordered to give up her seat to a white passenger. She refused and the white bus driver threatened to have her arrested. She refused again to move and was arrested. Because of her arrest, the entire African-American population of Montgomery boycotted the buses. Within a year, Montgomery's public transportation system was legally integrated. One of the most significant moments of the civil rights movement occurred because of *one* woman who refused to go to the back of the bus! You, too, can make a difference by setting an example to all those around you when you take positive steps toward being a person who appreciates diversity.

> ### Student Quote
>
> "Diversity cannot truly be promoted and fully realized unless people are aware of what is going on around them. Realize how lucky you are to have the things you have, and realize that many others do not have the same opportunities that are at your hands. Everyone plays a different part in society, and everyone contributes."
>
> —Brian Jacobs, political science major

THE WHOLE IN ONE

- Appreciation of diversity should be a goal for all of us. It's not enough to simply tolerate diversity.
- Diversity is not just drawn along racial lines. There are issues of diversity in gender, sexual orientation, citizenship, marital status, religious affiliation, and many other areas.
- In order to develop an appreciation of diversity, biases and prejudices must be owned up to, caught, and challenged, and everyone must be given the benefit of the doubt.
- There are many diversity and multicultural opportunities:
  - Learn a foreign language.
  - Take a course in cultural diversity.
  - Travel or study abroad.
  - Rent *Remember the Titans.*
- YOU can make a difference!

BECOME THE BEST YOU...APPRECIATE DIVERSITY!

Chapter 2 Review

Read each question and circle the *best* answer.

1. **Diversity is another way of saying**

   a. appreciation.

   b. respect.

   c. differences.

   d. culture.

2. **All of these are examples of appreciating diversity except**

   a. a computer company that develops products that have functionality for persons with disabilities.

   b. actively listening to someone about his/her culture and background.

   c. accepting and identifying your biases.

   d. being nice to a person of different culture to solidify your job status.

3. **"All blonde people are stupid" is**

   a. a prejudice.

   b. a stereotypical comment.

   c. a true statement.

   d. both a and b.

4. **What is the author's purpose for writing this chapter?**

   a. To define diversity

   b. To help prejudiced people

   c. To give people knowledge and strategies to appreciate diversity

   d. To get people involved in a multicultural experience

5. **Which expression would best pertain to this chapter?**

   a. Don't cry over spilled milk.

   b. Don't judge a book by its cover.

   c. Don't judge a person until you have walked a mile in his/her boots.

   d. Well done is better than well said.

6. **When you meet a person and feel a bias, you should**

   a. leave the area and end a possible conflict.

   b. go with the feeling.

   c. smile and talk nicely to the person.

   d. challenge the bias and give him/her a chance.

7. **The grandfather in "An Old Indian Grandfather" was trying to**

   a. teach his grandson how to exhibit a positive attitude.

   b. teach his grandson how to fight.

   c. teach his grandson how to focus his anger.

   d. do all of the above.

8. **What two words are synonyms?**

   a. Awareness/tolerance

   b. Bias/attitude

   c. Prejudice/anger

   d. Diversity/differences

9. **Which of these is an example of types of diversity found in the workplace?**

   a. Gender

   b. Race

   c. Hair color

   d. All of the above

10. **These are all examples of getting involved in multicultural experiences except**

    a. taking a foreign language class.

    b. studying abroad.

    c. paying attention on your class's field trips.

    d. taking a multicultural course.

Career and Character Education
Essential #3

Become a Team Player

"Lou Gerstner, Chairman and CEO of IBM, said, 'Integration is superior to isolation.' I've used this philosophy many times while speaking with students seeking full-time jobs or internships. (It's also at the bottom of all my e-mails.) It doesn't matter if you are a Technician or a Public Relations Specialist—defining a process or delivering a solution— a Team Project will be part of your career development. New employees that already embrace the concept of being a team player (there is no 'I' in team) will find that projects can be challenging and fun rather than frustrating and disruptive."

—IBM

What Is a Team Player?

If you are going to develop into the best you, being a team player is very important. To help us identify the essential qualities necessary to be a team player, let's take a look at a definition from the *New Webster's Dictionary and Thesaurus:*

> **Teamwork:** The quality whereby individuals unselfishly subordinate their own part to the general effort of the group with whom they are working or playing.

As we look at the definition of "teamwork," the key terms and phrases that stand out are *unselfish, subordinate their own part,* and *general effort of the group.* An essential quality of a good team is the ability to *work together* effectively towards a common goal. Another key quality is that the members of the team *believe in a common purpose or goal.*

Thus, using the key phrases and terms from the definition, here are four key qualities of a team player:

- Believes in the common goal of the team
- Works effectively together with other team members
- Is unselfish
- Subordinates his or her own part or self-interests for the betterment of the team

"Accenture seeks people who are team players because project team members must work together to achieve common goals for their clients. Being a good team player and sharing with colleagues contributes to the overall success of the project. We do not encourage people to work in a secluded environment but rather a collaborative environment where workload, ideas, and solutions can be shared."

—Accenture

Analyzing athletic teams has always been a good way to clearly see good teamwork in effect, because the *common purpose or goal* is easy to see: winning. Look at the following example that is based on a situation that actually occurred.

Missy and Alicia are two stars on their high school softball team. As seniors, they are playing the last game of their high school career today—the conference championship. Missy is an all-star shortstop who is one double play shy of the all-time conference record. Alicia is just three hits short of the team record for most hits in a season. The team they are playing against in the conference championship is famous for hitting the long ball, especially to left field. Unfortunately, the left fielder for the Greyhounds has a sprained knee and cannot play in the big game. Therefore, the coach approaches Missy and asks her to consider something: "Missy, I hate asking you to consider this, but our best chance of winning is to have you out in left field. This would blow your chance of getting the double-play record, but we need a strong arm in left field to win. I would completely understand if you want to stay at shortstop. It's your call." Missy thinks it over, but doesn't need much time. She has always put the team first. She informs the coach that she would be playing in left field during the championship game.

Missy unselfishly subordinated her self-interest of getting the individual record, because she believed in the common goal of the team: winning the championship.

The game was tight. It was 4-4 in the last inning, and the Greyhounds had a base runner on second base. Alicia was up to bat. She had already gotten two hits—just one shy of the record for most hits in a season. There were no outs, so the best thing to do would have been to advance the runner on second base to third base. This would allow the next batter to just have to hit a fly ball to get the base runner to score the winning run. The other team's infield was playing way back, knowing that Alicia usually hits the ball hard. Alicia knew that she could easily bunt the ball and advance the runner to third, but she would likely get out and not get her third hit. Alicia surprised everyone and bunted the ball. The pitcher got the ball and threw Alicia out at first, but the runner on second advanced to third. The next batter got a hit, and the Greyhounds won the championship.

Both Missy and Alicia understood what it meant to be team players. They sacrificed their own individual achievements for the team's common goal. You've probably heard the saying, "There is no 'I' in *Team*." It is becoming increasingly common in the workplace to be assigned to a team to complete various projects. In your career and in life, a big part of your success, then, will depend on how well you work within teams or how good of a team player you are. Additionally, you will remember from the previous chapter that the workplace is getting more diverse, so you must be able to work effectively with team members of different cultures and backgrounds.

"We deliver all of our services to our clients through the hard work of our teams. Teams are a critical part of our culture because we believe that teamwork drives excellence in our concepts and deliverables to our clients. Teams help to create environments where new thoughts and ideas are stimulated and embraced. Teams will work together to produce results that will take our client's business to the next level. Teams are able to support and drive each other to grow and develop."

—PricewaterhouseCoopers

How to Become a Team Player

There are many ways to become a team player. Here we will explore several of them, including using your interpersonal skills, learning how to effectively resolve conflicts, getting involved in extracurricular activities, and volunteering in the community.

Use Your Interpersonal Skills

To be a good team player, you have to be unselfish and willing to sacrifice yourself at times for the benefit of the team. In addition to these core team qualities, you obviously need to be able to relate well with your other team members. In other words, you must utilize the six underlying qualities of interpersonal skills presented in Chapter 1. That's the reason why "Become a People Person" (interpersonal skills) was the first Career and Character Education Essential presented in this book. Interpersonal skills are needed almost everywhere. Good interpersonal skills are necessary to work well with a wide variety of people (as seen in Chapter 2, "Appreciate Diversity") and to work well in teams. You will not be a good team player if you don't work constantly on your interpersonal skills.

> *Student Quote*
>
> "The minds of many put together are greater than the mind of one. Take advantage of opportunities to work in teams; it will help later on."
>
> —Brian Jacobs, political science major

"Individual contributors are an integral part of the company's make-up, but those individuals can be a part of many teams even if they have no reporting personnel. In other words, team players understand the impact of their work across the organization and the company. They do not work in a vacuum; their efforts are vertically integrated/streamlined into overarching company goals."

—Verizon

Learn to Resolve Conflicts Effectively

When you are part of a team for a substantial period, it's almost inevitable that conflicts between members will occur. Someone does something you feel is wrong or hurtful to the goal of the team. What do you do? Remain quiet so as not to "make waves"? Not if you are a team player. One of the most important qualities of a team player is the ability to confront others tactfully. Following are three steps that can help you turn confrontations into a positive outcome.

Step 1: Have the Courage to Confront

Too often people choose to avoid confrontation. It's not easy to confront someone; nobody likes friction in a group. However, when people don't confront one another, frustration with others often turns to resentment, and people start talking behind the backs of others. Ultimately, the team begins to splinter. Remember, a core quality of teamwork is to sacrifice your own self-interests for the benefit of the team. When you choose to avoid confrontation, you are keeping your own self-interests in mind—you don't want someone else to be mad at you. But by doing this, you're also disrespecting the person by talking behind his or her back and hurting the team in the process! Thus, the first step of confronting is to have enough "guts" to confront!

Step 2: Know WHERE and WHEN to Confront

The next step is to think about the most effective time and place to confront. If you have an issue with one person, it's usually best to approach that person individually. When you confront a person in front of a group, the person will naturally feel embarrassed and get defensive. You are putting that person on the spot and making other team members feel awkward. As for *when* to confront, don't do it if you are emotionally upset. It's best to give yourself time to cool down, think through what you want to say, and approach him or her later.

Step 3: Know HOW to Confront

When you do confront a team member, you want to do it as tactfully as you can. There is no benefit to belittling or offending him or her. You should think about what you want to say and choose your words wisely. Remember, the effects of hitting someone below the belt with a comment can last a very long time, as seen in the following story.

THE FENCE

There once was a little boy who had a bad temper. His father gave him a bag of nails and told him that every time he lost his temper, he must hammer a nail into the back of the fence.

The first day the boy had driven 37 nails into the fence. Over the next few weeks, as he learned to control his anger, the number of nails hammered daily gradually dwindled down. He discovered it was easier to hold his temper than to drive those nails into the fence.

Finally the day came when the boy didn't lose his temper at all. He told his father about it, and the father suggested that the boy now pull out one nail for each day that he was able to hold his temper.

The days passed, and the young boy was finally able to tell his father that all the nails were gone. The father took his son by the hand and led him to the fence. He said, "You have done well, my son, but look at the holes in the fence. The fence will never be the same. When you say things in anger, they leave a scar just like this one. You can put a knife in a man and draw it out. It won't matter how many times you say I'm sorry, the wound is still there. A verbal wound is as bad as a physical one."

—Author Unknown

Remember this story if you are one who speaks before thinking, especially if what you say could be hurtful. The way the conflict is resolved—and therefore the stability of the team—may depend largely on the way you approach the issue.

Examples of Resolving Conflicts

To illustrate this three-step process of resolving conflicts, let's take a look at both a bad and good example of resolving conflicts. Jessie and Reaney are participating in their school play. Jessie has been in many plays before and is really dedicated to theater. In fact, she plans on studying drama in college and becoming an actor someday. Reaney, on the other hand, is in her first play. She only wanted to be part of the play because her friend Emily was in it. Reaney and Emily spend a lot of the rehearsal time giggling and whispering to each other. As the night of the big play nears, Jessie's getting more and more frustrated with Reaney. It's getting harder for her to concentrate with Reaney and Emily messing around so much. Following are two different ways that Jessie confronts Reaney.

THE BAD EXAMPLE

As Jessie is rehearsing her lines with her classmate, Reaney and Emily begin giggling out loud. Jessie has had it! All of her pent up frustration must be relieved. She stops in the middle of saying her lines and yells at Reaney.

Jessie: Reaney, would you just shut up! I'm so sick of you giggling and messing around. You're acting like an idiot! Why did you even join this play in the first place?

Reaney: Oh just relax! What's the big deal? Who do you think you are, anyway?

Remember the three steps: Have the "guts" to confront, pick a good time and place to confront, and confront the person tactfully. Well, how did Jessie do? She did confront, but because she avoided confronting Reaney so many times before, Jessie bottled up a lot of frustration. That's why she exploded. Next, was this a good time and place to confront? No. Confronting Reaney in the middle of a rehearsal and in front of all their peers embarrassed Reaney and put her on the defensive. Finally, was Jessie tactful in how she confronted Reaney? Once again, no! Calling Reaney an idiot and telling her to shut up was not very tactful.

THE GOOD EXAMPLE

Jessie leaves several rehearsals feeling frustrated. She realizes something has to be said for the good of the play. She thinks about when and how to approach Reaney and decides to confront her after the next rehearsal. After the rehearsal is over, Jessie approaches Reaney and asks if she could talk to her for a minute.

Jessie: Reaney, I've been wanting to talk to you about something. I know these rehearsals get pretty long and boring at times, but I'm starting to worry about whether we'll be ready by opening night. I've been in other plays where we didn't prepare like we should have, and the play was a flop. I know that you and Emily are just trying to have a little fun, but frankly it gets a little tough to concentrate at times. I hope you don't mind me telling you this—I just want us to perform well.

Reaney: Gee, I'm sorry Jessie; I didn't realize we were bothering everybody. Emily and I will tone it down a bit.

Jessie: Thanks, Reaney—I really appreciate it.

Well, I think you can see that Jessie did a much better job of confronting the situation this time. She had enough courage to confront but chose to do it at a time when she was a bit more cooled down. She also wanted to confront Reaney one-on-one rather than in front of the group. And Jessie was much more tactful this time—she chose her words carefully and tried hard not to put Reaney on the defensive.

Get Involved in Extracurricular Activities

One of the best ways for you to develop your teamwork skills is to get involved in after-school activities, sports teams, and clubs. Make sure you get your hands on a list of the extracurricular activities that exist at your school. Joining the band, becoming a member of a play, or participating in sports allows you to experience being part of a team. You will learn the importance of working together and believing in a common goal. You'll gain experience dealing with conflicts and overcoming adversity. You'll see that when your team is successful, it's so much sweeter when you have teammates to share the success.

Regarding clubs, choose a club in which you are genuinely interested and start going to meetings. During the meetings, find out about the various events and programs your club offers, and determine in which ones you would like to get involved. Company and college recruiters say repeatedly that they want to hire graduates who were active in extracurricular activities and student clubs. It's not enough to just attend the meetings. See if there is a program or event that you can take a lead in coordinating. The experience you get as a member of a larger team (club) is good, but the work you do in smaller committees really gives you a good taste of teamwork.

Any time that you are part of a team, whether it is physical or mental, you are developing your teamwork skills. The key is to dive right in and give it a shot.

Volunteer in Your Community

As emphasized throughout this chapter, a big part of being a team player is being unselfish and sacrificing your own agenda to benefit the larger team. This is really the essence of community service. Your local community is a type of team, and certain members of this team or community are not as fortunate in life as you are. Giving of yourself and volunteering your time for the benefit of others in need is being the ultimate team player!

> ### Student Quote
>
> "Know your strengths and weaknesses. Volunteer to be a team leader when your strengths apply to the problem being solved. Be an active participant and let someone else take the role of leader if his/her strengths compliment your weaknesses."
>
> —Kristi Geist, management major

Know Your In-Group Tendencies and Adjust

No matter what team you are a member of, as you work in groups—especially during the many meetings of which you will be a part—be aware of your interpersonal tendencies. Do you tend to talk a lot in groups, or do you hardly say anything? Are you more of a big-picture, bottom-line type of person, or do you like to work out the details? A crucial part of being a team player is to understand your natural tendencies and adjust accordingly for the benefit of the group. For example, if you are an extrovert and tend to answer many of the questions and dominate a lot of the discussion during meetings or in class, you should intentionally keep yourself from talking at times so that others have a chance to contribute their views. Pick the issues about which you feel strongly, and let other team or class members contribute and offer their perspectives. Similarly, if you tend to be a big-picture person with hundreds of ideas, you may need to force yourself to offer just a few and focus in on the details of carrying out the ideas.

To summarize, being a team player means that you will be aware of the entire team and its members, own up to your natural tendencies, and adjust your behavior to benefit the team.

THE WHOLE IN ONE

- Top company recruiters reinforce the importance of teamwork in the 21st-century organization.
- The essential qualities of a team player are working together towards a common goal and sacrificing your own best interests to serve the greater good of the team.
- Strong interpersonal skills are a must for the effective team player.
- Confrontation gets a bad rap. When handled tactfully, it can be a powerful way to move past hurdles and work together more effectively.
- Extracurricular activities and community service are great ways to build your teamwork skills.
- Natural interpersonal tendencies may need to be adjusted to benefit the committee or team.

BECOME THE BEST YOU...BECOME A TEAM PLAYER!

Chapter 3 Review

Read each question and circle the *best* answer.

1. **What quality in a person is the most important to be a team player?**

   a. Bravery

   b. Unselfishness

   c. Intelligence

   d. Good communication skills

2. **To be a great team player, it is crucial that a person consistently works on**

   a. communication skills.

   b. physical appearance.

   c. interpersonal skills.

   d. public speaking.

3. **When a teammate is doing something that is hurting the team, a good example of tactfully confronting the teammate would be,**

   a. "I hear what you are saying but here is what we are going to do."

   b. "You're wrong and I'll tell you why."

   c. "You are not thinking of the team. You are all about you."

   d. "That's a good idea, but what do you think of this one?"

4. **The best time to confront a person is when**

   a. you are upset.

   b. you are in a group situation.

   c. you are in front of the entire class.

   d. you are one-on-one with that person.

5. **The purpose for including "The Fence" in Chapter 3 was to show**

   a. how one should build a fence.

   b. how one should control his/her anger.

   c. that it is okay to lose your temper sometimes.

   d. that one should think before speaking.

6. **The dialogue between Reaney and Jessie was used to show**

    a. how to pick a fight properly.

    b. how to tactfully handle a conflict.

    c. how nice people should talk to one another.

    d. that the best time to confront someone is in a group setting.

7. **The author states that the ultimate team player is one who participates in**

    a. extracurricular activities.

    b. community service.

    c. conflicts.

    d. part-time jobs.

8. **Regarding extracurricular activities, college and company recruiters believe you should**

    a. choose a well-respected activity.

    b. become the president of the club or organization.

    c. become active in your chosen club or organization.

    d. attend meetings.

9. **A crucial part of being a team player is to understand your natural tendencies and**

    a. use them to the best of your ability.

    b. adjust them for the benefit of the group.

    c. change them totally for the benefit of the group.

    d. do the complete opposite.

4

Career and Character Education Essential #4

Manage Adversity

"One person a long time ago said that what doesn't kill you makes you stronger. This is true now more than ever. It does not take much integrity or character to handle life when everything is going your way. What sets winners apart from everyone else is how they handle defeat. It is in defeat that you find out what people are made of."

—Enterprise Rent-A-Car

How Can I Manage Adversity and Become a Person of Character?

What do you think of when you hear the term "character"? Maybe a more important question is *who* do you think of when you hear the term "character"? Now realize—I'm not talking about those people to whom we sarcastically refer as being "quite a character"—*That Erik is funny, he is quite a character!* No, I'm talking about people who consistently *show a lot of character* by fighting through adversity, maintaining a positive attitude even when things aren't going their way, and dealing effectively with people who are difficult to be around. I discuss these three underlying qualities that help manage adversity and define a person of strong character.

1. Fight Through Adversity and Define Your Character

As the great late Green Bay Packer coach Vince Lombardi said, "When the going gets tough, the tough get going!" There is no better indicator of character than how you deal with adversity. I'm sure at one point or another you've heard a sports announcer say, "He showed a lot of character after losing the big game." Anybody can be a great person when things are going well. But when you stare into the face of adversity— flunking a test, losing a big game, having your girlfriend/boyfriend break up with you—this is the true test of character. How you come back and perform in these tough times defines your character. So when adversity comes your way, approach it as an opportunity to showcase the kind of person you are. When you think about it, you have two choices: fight or flight. If you are a person of character, you will fight through the disappointments and setbacks and show the world how much character you have.

"Upon entering the Army, a soldier takes an oath swearing or affirming that he or she 'will support and defend the Constitution of the United States against all enemies, foreign and domestic....' Implied in that oath is the willingness to face and conquer any and all adversity in the fulfillment of that oath. Minor adversities might include fatigue and sleep, food, and water deprivation. The ultimate adversity involves life and death. It is important to the Army to enlist recruits who know the adversities they may face."

—Colonel Art Bair (Retired), U.S. Army

Remember when you were three or four years old, and you always seemed to win all the games you played? Your parents or older brother or sister would intentionally lose so you could win. Well, since that time, it hasn't been that easy, right? I'm sure you've experienced your share of losing just as the rest of us have. Everybody in this world experiences failure from time to time. But why is it that some people are able to "roll with the punches" better than others? You know who I mean—those people who are able to "get right back on that horse" after a major disappointment or setback. The following are two pointers to help you deal with setbacks.

Accept the Nature of the Game

People who deal best with adversity have accepted the fact that losing is a part of life—and that, in losing, there's an opportunity to learn and become better. I'm not suggesting that you go into a new situation or game hoping to lose so you can become better. I believe that being competitive and pushing hard to win is necessary for success in life. What I am suggesting is that you learn to analyze the situations you're in and accept the nature of those situations. It's about getting a realistic mindset. Let me illustrate the point using a baseball hitter.

Think about baseball hitters. When they get one hit out of three times at bat, it's been a good day, right? Major leaguers go home happy after going one out of three at the plate. But wait—if you really stop and analyze this, you'll see that they have failed two out of three times at bat! How can they go home happy when they failed two out of three times? They can be happy because they've accepted the nature of the game. A .333 batting average (one out of three) is universally accepted in the baseball world as a good, respectable average.

As you throw yourself out there—trying for the lead in your school's play, running for vice president of your class, studying to get an "A," or trying out for a team sport—learn to accept the nature of the game. Some things are more competitive and more difficult to win than others. This is a very important concept to grasp before you start applying to college or begin looking for your first job. You see, a typical job search goes something like this: no, no, no, no, no, no, no, no, no, no, no, no, no, no, no, no, no, no, no, no, no, no, YES! That one yes is all you need to get a job. However, the hard part for most job seekers is getting through the *no's*! If you stop job searching because of the rejections you experience, you'll never get a job. Thus a key to success in finding a job is having a type of mind set that prepares you to accept the nature of the job search game: You will be rejected many more times than you are accepted, but you need to get accepted only once. So, remember to keep things in perspective, take the setbacks in stride, and get right back on the horse that threw you!

> ### Student Quote
>
> "Putting yourself in an uncomfortable situation, like working with senior citizens or small children for the first time, will really improve your character. I started visiting retirement centers in the beginning of high school, and it was really awkward at first, but by the end of senior year I went to every visit I could go to."
>
> —Michelle Kelly, education major

Always Believe in Yourself

A second pointer in being able to fight through adversity has to do with your level of self-confidence. Those who are able to overcome obstacles never stop believing in themselves. If you are true to yourself and believe in what you're trying to accomplish in life, you will be able to get through setbacks. Focus more on reaching your destination and not on the little potholes along the way. You must have enough confidence in yourself to think things through, form your own opinions and beliefs, and act on those beliefs. When you begin doubting yourself after experiencing failure, it is much harder to get through adversity and ultimately become successful. There is no quick and easy way to build your self-confidence. It really boils down to knowing and accepting who you are, believing in yourself, and being optimistic. Maintaining a positive attitude toward life and yourself is critical to being self-confident and getting through the hard times.

2. Be a Big Person and Remain Positive

"The best way to look at life is that it is full of choices. Everyday we choose to wake up, get out of bed, and go on with our day. What you cannot choose is what happens *to you*. A speaker once described change as a moving train. You can do three things: Stand in front of it and get run over—this is what happens to negative people. You can stand beside the tracks and watch it go by—much like people that say, 'That doesn't or won't affect me,' and they miss their opportunity. Or you can do what I advocate: Jump on board and see where it takes you. You must always search for the positive and downplay the negative. Remember, it is your choice. You can smile or frown. Anger takes your energy while happiness gives you energy."

—Enterprise Rent-A-Car

Another underlying personal quality that goes hand-in-hand with strong character is being a big person and having a positive attitude. Nobody likes to hang around petty people who are always whining and being negative. To be a person of character, you should try to look at the glass as being half full rather than half empty. It's easy to fall into the glass-half-empty trap when you have so much on your plate and you're feeling tired. However, when you are able to stay upbeat, you'll be surprised how much positive energy you'll have. Following are three pointers to help you stay positive.

Rise Above the Little Things

Don't make too big of a deal over the little things; keep them in perspective. We all have a tendency to stress out over many little things going on in our lives. We have to learn to tell ourselves to rise above it and just *let it be*. Do any of the following statements ring a bell?

"I think she's mad at me for some reason. I wonder what I did?"

"Why does he always do that? It's so annoying."

"My parents are being so hard on me lately. They need to relax."

The little things that happen to you can turn into a bigger deal when you don't just let it be. Whether or not you drive, you can relate to a very common little thing that has turned into a big deal for many people: Someone pulls out in front of you when driving.

When someone pulls out in front of you when you are driving, you have two options. Option one is doing what many people do: Speed up and ride the bumper of the person who cut you off, beep your horn repetitively, and make obscene hand gestures. Option two is to just let it be. When you choose the first option, think about how it affects you. Usually the other driver gets angry and retaliates in some fashion. This causes you to get even angrier than you originally were when he pulled out in front of you. Aside from the fact that you are now encouraging a fight and risking your life, you have worked yourself into a frenzy.

Is it really worth all this? Because somebody (who you don't even know) pulled out in front of you and made you slow down a little, your blood is boiling, you are yelling obscenities that only you can hear, and you are risking your life and the lives of others around you. And it usually doesn't end when you park your car. What do you do with that anger? You take it with you. So now you are a bit edgier and angrier for the next few hours, while you relive this event in your head and tell your friends about it. Little things can really add up and eat away at your positive energy.

> *Student Quote*
>
> "Take a sincere interest in those around you. People feel better about themselves when others are interested in them. If people feel good around you, you will be trusted and liked by most everyone."
>
> —*Kristi Geist, management major*

On the other hand, if you had chosen the second option and just let it be, think how much better off you'd be. It's surprising how good you feel when you let it be. Remember, it's easy to let yourself get angry in these situations. It takes a much more positive, secure person with strong character to just let it be. Don't let the little things affect the attitude you portray to the world!

Don't Stress over Being Busy

You can probably relate to at least one of the following statements.

> "How am I ever going to be ready for that test?"
>
> "I can't possibly get all this done by next Friday."
>
> "Today is a nightmare. Right after school, I have to run to practice. Then, right after practice, I have to meet up with my study group. And then, somehow, I have to find time to write my reaction paper that's due tomorrow morning."

Don't you get tired of people who always seem to be running around and telling everyone how busy they are? Who is *not* busy? To remain positive, you must accept the fact that you are going to be busy. It can undoubtedly be stressful for you when you're multitasking, but there are ways to deal with it. While telling everyone that you're busy may relieve a tiny bit of stress, it doesn't help your sense of character fare well. It's just not worth it. The best thing you can do to alleviate some of the stress associated with being busy is to stay organized. When you spend a few minutes each day prioritizing your tasks and preparing for the day, you'll be able to take things in stride, one thing at a time.

Take Care of Yourself Physically

A big part of being positive starts with how you feel physically. A psychologist once said, "You are a different person when you're not tired." I know, it's not the most profound statement, but it may be one of the most underrated ones. When you're tired, everything seems a bit more dreary and negative, doesn't it? Why are babies so happy and positive right after they nap, yet so cranky right before bedtime?

It's also important to exercise and have some alone time. Exercising is a great way to relieve stress and clear your head. Also, try to spend even just a half-hour each day by yourself. Take a walk, hang out and listen to music, or just lie on your bed. As a student (and later as a businessperson), you interact with many people for a good chunk of the day. It's healthy to take a break occasionally and reintroduce recess into your life!

3. Deal Effectively with Difficult People

"Let's face it, it's much easier to say (and they may even mean it) that they value diversity and are open to working with a variety of coworkers—even those who are most difficult to work with—but it is a whole different ballgame when it comes to being able to listen to different perspectives from challenging employees and subsequently disseminate those values and experiences into a resolution that is acceptable to parties from various constituencies."

—Smart & Associates

The final success factor to managing adversity concerns how you deal with people who are difficult to be around. You might be the most positive person in the world, but that won't always keep you from crossing paths with classmates, teammates, teachers, coaches, and other people who aren't very positive and who are a pain to deal with. Dealing with difficult people can be challenging; it takes a lot of character to be able to interact well with difficult people. Following are a few strategies to help you cope more effectively with people who are tough to be around.

Don't Take Things Personally and Become Defensive

The most natural, knee-jerk reaction to people who are being a pain in the butt is to get mad and become defensive. Do any of these responses sound familiar?

"Who do you think you are?"

"It's not my problem—you're the one being a jerk about it."

"Why do you have to be such an idiot all of the time?"

The problem with this approach is that "two wrongs don't make a right." Yes, sometimes people's behavior needs to be addressed, but there is a better way to do it. For starters, when dealing with difficult people, try not to take things so personally. Difficult people tend to be negative to everybody—they're not singling you out. When you become defensive and strike back, it typically fuels their fire.

One of the truest measures of strength and character is the ability to take the high road when confronted by a negative, cynical, mean-spirited person. Conversely, it's a sign of weakness if you're lured into petty arguments or trash talking. People of character are able to take difficult people with a grain of salt and (internally) laugh off the bullies of the world. In other words, don't stoop to their level; rise above and don't let them get to you!

Don't Hide from or Avoid Difficult People

"A young paratrooper standing in the door of an aircraft in flight about 1,200 feet above the ground has a split second to overcome the fear he may feel before jumping from that aircraft while having complete faith in his parachute. Having exited the aircraft as trained is a sign of his facing and conquering adversity."

—Colonel Art Bair (Retired), U.S. Army

Another common reaction to difficult people is avoidance. Many people simply try hard to duck or avoid people who are a pain to be around. No doubt, this is the "path of least resistance," but people of character don't take the easiest way out—they do the right thing. And the right thing is to never write off any human being.

In the world of work, it can be especially difficult to avoid confrontation. Often you'll be assigned to a committee or project team, and your success will depend on the success of the group. Avoiding difficult coworkers in such situations will often be counterproductive.

To further illustrate the importance of not quitting on people you don't enjoy being around, let's look at this example of an important lesson a youth counselor learned.

Student Quote

"I am a firm believer that 'what doesn't kill you will only make you stronger.' Through the challenges of any adverse situation, a student will learn something about his or her character. By seeking opportunities to challenge oneself in high school, students will have a firm grasp on their character once they enter college and be able to refine their personality traits to better fit their individualized career goals."

—*Jennifer Watkavitch, recent graduate*

Jennifer was a first-year counselor at a youth clinic. Part of her on-the-job training was to have her counseling sessions videotaped and critiqued by her supervisor. Well, Jennifer had five clients (children). Four out of the five were fairly easy to work with; they had their issues, but they respected Jennifer and listened to what she advised. Mike, however, was cynical and challenged much of what Jennifer had to say. When reviewing the videotapes, the supervisor noticed that Jennifer's energy level was considerably lower when working with Mike than with the other four clients. Jennifer consistently ended sessions with Mike early and even rescheduled a couple sessions altogether. At the midyear review, Jennifer received a low score on her formal evaluation from her supervisor. Jennifer felt that the supervisor was being unfair and confronted him.

Jennifer: I don't agree with the score you gave me on my evaluation. I've worked hard over the last six months, and four out of the five clients have really grown since I've been working with them. I can't help it if one of my clients isn't willing to take any of my suggestions!

(continued)

(continued)

> **Supervisor:** Jennifer, I gave you a low score because I felt that you quit on Mike. You didn't give him the same time or energy as your other clients. You were aware of Mike's background, and you even said early on that you felt like Mike was dealt a really bad hand. In my opinion, Mike needed counseling more than any of your other clients and had the biggest potential for improvement. You see, Jen, a true professional is one who is able to face adversity and generate positive energy when working with the most difficult clients. Any counselor can coach somebody who is accommodating and agreeable.

Similar to what Jennifer learned, we all need to remember that it's easy to be a positive person of strong character when surrounded by accommodating, friendly people; it's how you respond to angry, negative, difficult people that defines you and your character. Rather than avoid difficult people, think of it as an opportunity to help a fellow human being in need and show the kind of person you are, and maybe even the kind of person they *could* be.

"Fold your tent or suck it up and work harder and smarter. 'When the going gets tough, the tough get going.' Look at it as a golden opportunity to prove you can handle adversity and come out on top!"

—Top Sales Rep Mike Logan (Retired), Pfizer

Pick Your Battles and Confront Individually

Try not to overreact to difficult people. Hang in there and try to stay positive. However, there will be times when you've tried everything and nothing is working. Since I don't believe in quitting on anybody, a last resort is to confront the difficult person individually. When you do so, remember not to call them out in public. It's always best to address your concerns one-on-one. Also remember to be sensitive and tactful; you won't get anywhere if you upset them and put them on the defensive. Finally, start off by explaining that you care about them, and that's why you wanted to talk to them about something that's been bothering you. When people believe that you care about them, they're much more likely to be more receptive.

When you do confront them, be sure to stick to the matter at hand. Address your concerns honestly, but be sure to give the other person space to share his or her thoughts and feelings. Remember that most disagreements are handled through compromise. Also remember that one true test of a person's character is his or her ability to see and sympathize with others' points of view.

In summary, a person of character is best defined by those moments of adversity. What are those tough situations and difficult people that tend to challenge your character? How can you respond differently next time around to become a stronger person of character?

THE WHOLE IN ONE

- The true test of one's character is how one deals with adversity. You have to have the right mindset to persevere, and you should always believe in yourself.

- You must be a big person and remain positive. Specifically, you should rise above the petty things, don't stress so much over being busy, and take care of yourself physically.

- One of the toughest forms of facing adversity is dealing with difficult people. To become a person of character, you must challenge yourself to deal directly with difficult people, to not get defensive, and to confront them in a respectful, caring way!

BECOME THE BEST YOU...MANAGE ADVERSITY!

Chapter 4 Review

Read each question and circle the *best* answer.

1. **Enterprise Rent-A-Car states that what sets winners apart from everyone else is how they handle**

   a. victory.

   b. defeat.

   c. themselves.

   d. their team.

2. **The best way to define *facing adversity* would be**

   a. how a person handles a tough situation.

   b. how a person argues a point.

   c. how a person asks questions.

   d. how a person relates with positive people.

3. **What does "When the going gets tough, the tough get going" mean?**

   a. When times are tough, leave the situation.

   b. When tough people leave you, you must get tough.

   c. In a difficult situation, people with character stand up to the challenge.

   d. When facing a tough situation, people with character go to an easier one.

4. **In order to face adversity in the most positive way, you must first learn to**

   a. deal with people.

   b. be a good loser.

   c. be a boastful winner.

   d. accept that you'll fail sometimes and learn from it.

5. **One way to help with "busy" stress is to**

   a. get help.

   b. get organized.

   c. get a friend.

   d. get out of the situations that make you so busy.

6. **The first thing to do when interacting with difficult people is to**

    a. avoid them.
    b. not take it personally.
    c. confront them.
    d. talk to other people about them.

7. **When is it best to avoid difficult people?**

    a. Always
    b. When they lie
    c. Never
    d. When they become argumentative

8. **When you are confronting a difficult person, do all of the following except**

    a. tell them they must stop what they're doing.
    b. tell them that you care about them.
    c. avoid confronting them in public.
    d. avoid putting them on the defensive.

9. **A true professional, based on the example of the counselor, is somebody who**

    a. maintains the same level of positive energy with difficult people.
    b. is the best in their field.
    c. is constantly learning new things.
    d. maintains a positive attitude with people of all ages and races.

10. **All of these are necessary qualities of a person of character except for being**

    a. intelligent.
    b. positive.
    c. resilient.
    d. sensitive.

Career and Character Education
Essential #5

Communicate Effectively

"Accenture works with clients to solve their business challenges and provide solutions for their continued success. We seek individuals who possess strong written and verbal communication skills because they will be key attributes in gathering information, analyzing and relaying that information, and reaching end solutions for teams internally as well as for our clients."

—Accenture

Communication in the Modern World

"Communication skills are utilized every day. Whatever the medium—be it face-to-face meetings, written correspondence, conference calls, etc.—employees are engaged in communication. Employees face an endless exchange of ideas, messages, and information as they deal with one another and with customers day after day. How well they communicate can determine whether a company quickly grows into an industry leader or joins thousands of other businesses mired in mediocrity."

—Verizon

Important to becoming the best you is being a good communicator. That means being comfortable with your language, whether you are writing, reading, speaking, or listening to it. Before we learn how to communicate more effectively, let's look at all the different means of communication that are utilized in the 21st century workplace and in our world today.

In Person

- One-on-one verbal conversations
- One-on-one sign language
- Small-group facilitation and workshops
- Small-group meetings
- Large-group verbal presentations and speeches
- Large-group presentations and speeches via sign language
- Large-group social gatherings

Telephone

- Traditional one-on-one conversations
- Teleconferencing (more than two people)
- Speaker phones
- Mobile/cell phones
- Texting

Student Quote

"Communication skills are vital in setting you apart from everyone else. These skills should be developed and practiced in high school and college because they are the resource that is going to further your career. I suggest obtaining an internship in your field of interest or getting a part-time job working with the public that will help to hone and sharpen your communication skills."

—Michelle Ford,
communication arts major

Writing

- Handwritten letters and memos
- Typed letters and documents
- E-mail messages (and attachments)
- Internet chatting
- Multimedia presentation writing
- Web page documents
- Blogging

Audio/Video

- Videoconferencing (talking and observing)
- Video interviewing (interviewing candidates via videoconferencing)
- Electronic video clips (sent via Internet)
- Podcasting
- Social networking sites (MySpace/Facebook)

You have likely identified a means of communication that I forgot to add. However, this list still illustrates the point that we have the ability to communicate in so many different ways, all over the world, instantaneously. The ability to communicate effectively becomes more important as we expand our communication capabilities.

"Employees must be able to communicate effectively in e-mail through an innate understanding of the unique communications challenges of this medium. E-mail requires careful, thoughtful communication for tone, style, etc. If these considerations are not effectively managed, employees run the risk of having their e-mail messages misinterpreted, which creates conflict and slows a team's progress in achieving its goals."

—Microsoft

Improving Your Communication Skills

Developing strong communication skills is critical to becoming the best you. When you communicate, you reveal the type of person you are and people form an impression of you based on the way you communicate. For example, when you write a clear and fluent letter, people perceive you as intelligent. If you swear or use crude language, people think of you as "rough around the edges." When you yell and are nasty to others, people get the impression that you're mean. You see, the way you communicate speaks volumes to the type of person you are perceived to be. To develop your communication skills, you must learn how to write well and sharpen your verbal skills.

Learn How to Write Well

Recruiters frequently tell career counselors the importance they place upon good writing skills when hiring graduates. They have witnessed poor writing skills too often in young employees. It is not only that the business documents were not crafted well, but also that the documents were unclear and contained numerous grammatical errors. There is truly an art to writing, and it does not come naturally to most. However, as with any skill, the more you practice and gain experience in writing, the better you will become.

The most common first impression you give to college and company recruiters comes from the *cover letter* that you submit along with your application or resume. A cover letter is a one-page letter that serves to introduce you and your application to a potential employer. It is the first opportunity you get to demonstrate your writing skills to a prospective employer or college admissions officer. To give you a better feel for what we mean by good writing skills, look at the following two sample cover letters written by a college senior.

> ### Student Quote
>
> "Whether you are pursuing a career in biology or social services, you still must be able to communicate with the people around you. There is no occupation in which a person never has to communicate with their peers, so it is important that you start to gain your communication skills in high school."
>
> —Kim Brown,
> recent graduate

COVER LETTER SAMPLE #1

333 Charles Lane
Littlestown, PA 11111
January 15, 2009

Ms. Anne Mummert
Recruiting Manager
Koontz Consulting
1601 Timothy Lane
Philadelphia, PA 19103

Dear Ms. Mummert:

I am a senior at Bair College and would like a job at Koontz Consulting. I know I have the skills that you're looking for. I am a hard worker and can just about get along with everybody. My experience at Werner & Associates gave me a lot of good skills. I think I have what it takes to be successful.

Your company is just what I'm looking for. I want a well-established company who works good with a wide range of clients. I also want to work for a company that will allow me to grow and advance fast. I think I can learn good and move up quick. I'm highly motivated too. And I'm well-rounded.

If you need to get in touch, just give me a ring. I'll expect to hear from you soon. Thanks.

Sincerely,

Bo Brent

COVER LETTER SAMPLE #2

333 Charles Lane
Littlestown, PA 11111
January 15, 2009

Ms. Anne Mummert
Recruiting Manager
Koontz Consulting
1601 Timothy Lane
Philadelphia, PA 19103

Dear Ms. Mummert:

I am writing to express my interest in pursuing consulting opportunities at Koontz Consulting. After reviewing your Web page and reading your annual report, I am very excited about the possibility of working as a consultant for Koontz Consulting. The emphases on developing a world-class team, creating a lasting positive change, and providing excellent client services are particularly attractive. Furthermore, I am committed to using my consulting skills in the dynamic and ever-changing private sector. I believe that my abilities and interests match these values, as demonstrated by my resume.

Through my relevant professional experience and my work in strategic planning, change management, and organization development, I have gained the knowledge, experience, skills, and self-confidence to help empower companies to reach higher levels of productivity and efficiency that lasts. I am confident that my prior experience in facilitating strategic planning sessions, training organizations on computer applications and budgeting, and leading research projects on topics including transport logistics and customer service has provided me with the skills needed to become a successful consultant at Koontz Consulting.

I have enclosed a copy of my resume for you to review. I would greatly appreciate the opportunity to learn more about Koontz Consulting and its various professional opportunities. I will call you next week to see if there may be a convenient time to meet with you. Thank you for your time and consideration.

Sincerely,

Bo Brent

It is readily apparent that the second sample is considerably stronger than the first one. The first cover letter is written poorly, contains bad grammar, and lacks fluidity, which means the points do not flow well from one to the next. Additionally, the job candidate does not give a compelling enough explanation for his stated desire to work for Koontz Consulting. It is excessively vague. Do you see how the second cover letter flows much more smoothly? Bo better explains why he wants to work for Koontz, and he is specific about his past experience. Furthermore, he shows a greater connection between his abilities and the needs of the company.

One Word, Even One Letter, Can *Ruin* a First Impression

It is critical that you always go back, reread, and edit your written work. Online spell-check systems will catch words that are spelled incorrectly, but they don't catch words that you were not intending to use. The following is one of the biggest resume bloopers of all time:

What was intended: Responsible for **running** the entire Northeast chain of restaurants.

What was written: Responsible for **ruining** the entire Northeast chain of restaurants.

One letter—an "i" instead of an "n"—gave this line on the resume a whole new meaning. Have someone else who has a critical eye read over important documents you send out.

How to Develop Your Writing Skills

As was noted previously, writing is a skill, and as all skills go, the more you practice, the better you become. Following are some ways that you can develop your writing skills while in school.

Take English and Literature Classes

Most schools require that you take at least one course in English or literature per year. In addition to the requirements, seek out additional courses that relate to English and writing.

Pick Writing-Intensive Courses and Challenging English Teachers

Though most students seek to discover which courses are easiest and which teachers are least demanding, you will benefit more if you do the opposite. You can go with the flow, or you can choose to swim upstream. Look at it this way: Either you pay now, or you pay later. If you choose the courses that do not challenge your writing ability now, you will pay later when you are on the job or in college and cannot put together a well-written letter or report.

Think about the tough courses you've previously had in school. Those tough courses made it easier on you when you took the same subject the next year. If you have a tough teacher in pre-calculus, for example, the calculus course you'll have to take will probably seem that much easier. If your Spanish I teacher had high expectations, Spanish II won't be so difficult. Pick the tough teachers and writing-intensive courses now to help you develop the writing skills you will need later in your career and life.

Use Your School or Local Writing Tutors

Some schools have writing tutors available to help you write your papers more effectively. If not, check out a local learning center that offers tutoring help in writing, or ask an older sister, brother, or classmate to take a look at your papers. Just as it is a great idea for a beginning golfer to take lessons from a golf instructor, it is a good idea for young writers to take lessons from a writing tutor. The tutor will offer writing techniques that speed up the learning process. Plus, your grades will likely improve because your papers will be of a higher quality.

Read, Read, and Read Some More

"Communication—both written and verbal—allows understanding and being understood. It's not only important to have great people skills and relationship skills but equally important to be able to communicate with individuals who prefer to see it on paper as opposed to hearing it."

—Jefferson Pilot

Reading books and articles exposes you to various writing styles. In essence, the authors are serving as writing models for you. It is similar to learning how to speak. Children who speak well and intelligently usually have parents who have spoken well and modeled good verbal communication skills. Conversely, parents who have limited vocabularies often raise children who have similar limited vocabularies. The more that you read high-quality books and journal articles, the more modeling you will receive. This is a process that takes place without you, the reader, even realizing it. As you read, you see firsthand how to express your thoughts more fluently and articulately, and there will be a carryover into your writing.

Sharpen Your Verbal Communication Skills

"Our employees spend a great deal of their time working with customers, interacting and working closely with their colleagues, marketing their business, and representing Enterprise in their community. Therefore, it is vital that our employees have strong communication skills."

—Enterprise Rent-A-Car

Writing well does not come easily, but at least in writing, if you make a mistake or cannot think of the right words to use, you can take time and edit your first draft. However, when it comes to expressing yourself verbally, you usually don't get a second draft. Just as the cover letter is the first time you'll demonstrate your writing skills to company recruiters, the interview is the first time you'll demonstrate your verbal communication skills. Try to envision yourself on your first interview—even if it is a long time away. Following are the exact words from part of a videotaped mock (practice) interview of a college senior.

Interviewer: What are your greatest strengths?

Senior: Well, like, I'm a good communicator, and, um, I am, like, pretty dependable. Um, like, I feel that, um, oh, um, I can get along with, like, anybody. Um, um, I, um, also think, um, um, I, well, I know I can get the job done good.

As you can tell, it is not easy for most students to express their thoughts while sounding somewhat professional. When you are talking to your friends, you have the luxury of not worrying about how you talk to them. However, speaking casually with friends can cause you to develop bad speaking habits. It is easy to get a little sloppy and lazy with how you express yourself on a day-to-day basis, because most of the time you are not being judged on how you talk. In your life, though, there will be many times when you have to take it up a notch—when you want to make a good impression by saying the right thing in the right way. Following are some of the ways for you to practice speaking and work on your verbal communication skills.

Take Speech Communication Courses

Many high schools offer some kind of speech communication course. It may be disguised in some fancy new catchphrase, so you may need to ask your school counselor. If a course is not offered, see if you could take a similar course at your area community college. This type of course teaches you the primary techniques that are used to enhance your verbal communication skills. The course also gives you opportunities to practice speaking to your peers and to receive critical feedback from your teacher. Take the course—it's a no-brainer.

Seek Out In-Class Opportunities

Within your classes, there are frequently opportunities to speak to the class on various topics. Sometimes class presentations are structured into your class. Take these assignments seriously and use them as an opportunity to improve your verbal skills. However, there are other less formal times when the teacher simply asks for volunteers to answer questions or talk about various topics or assignments. Jump right in and volunteer.

Become a Leader

Another great reason to pursue leadership opportunities (besides developing your leadership skills) is to work on your speaking skills. As a leader of a club or team, you will be responsible for leading meetings and speaking on behalf of the team. This is a great way to enhance your verbal communication skills in more of a structured setting. You will also be asked to give speeches to various other groups regarding your club's mission and activities. Most leaders serve this public relations role and give many speeches. You will learn about many additional benefits of being a leader in Chapter 8!

Student Quote

"Communicating with others is one of the most important and difficult skills to master. I constantly have to refine how I communicate with others because each encounter with others brings about a unique difference, which changes how I need to communicate. For example, when I speak to my college roommates, I do not shake their hand firmly and ensure I make direct eye contact, but when the regional vice president for the company I work for comes in my building I do just that."

—*Ellery Loomis, recent graduate*

Practice Communicating During Part-Time Jobs

When you are at your part-time or summer job, you typically are among peers, but it is likely that you are also among full-time professional workers. You may have to deal with customers on a daily basis. This is a great opportunity for you to practice communicating more professionally. Take your part-time jobs seriously and put some effort into how you express your thoughts to coworkers and customers. Seek out leadership opportunities by volunteering to train new workers. Verbal communication skills are tested when you are training others.

Participate in Speech Communication Seminars

Keep your eye out for communication workshops or seminars that are offered by area businesses or your local community center. These workshops are designed to teach you the proper ways of communicating and how you can enhance your communication skills. Call your area Chamber of Commerce to see if they offer or are aware of any business communication seminars.

Critique Yourself on Video

There is no finer verbal-communication training than watching yourself speak. If your school doesn't offer this type of thing, borrow your parents' video camera and tape yourself giving a presentation you've done for class or will be doing. Okay, it may seem a little weird, but if you're serious about enhancing your communication skills, this is the way to go! Think about it: What other chance do you have of observing your nonverbal communication skills and listening to your verbal communication? Oh sure, you probably watch yourself on videos messing around at a picnic or during holidays. However, that's a little different. When you watch yourself in action while giving a speech, you are seeing how you communicate in more of a professional setting.

> **Student Quote**
>
> "To be an effective communicator, you have to first be an effective listener. Hearing the message of those you are working with is the solution to decreasing tension among peers, whether you're working with someone in the classroom or in the workplace. Becoming a better listener in the classroom will also make the transition to college easier."
>
> —*Jennifer Watkavitch, recent graduate*

Face Your Fear of Public Speaking

It's important that you work on developing your verbal communication skills while you are still in school, so that when it is time to graduate, you will be in better shape than our senior mock-interviewing friend was. However, many students avoid speaking in front of others due to anxiety and fear. It is very common to get nervous and somewhat anxious about public speaking. Here are some points to remember in dealing with your anxiety:

- **Take heart in knowing you are not alone.** Many people experience anxiety toward public speaking. In surveys conducted on things people fear, "speaking in front of a group" often ranks up there in the top few.

- **You are your toughest critic.** Think about how you feel when others are speaking. You are barely listening, and you're not judging them critically. You're probably daydreaming through some of their presentation. It is not that big of a deal to the people sitting in their seats watching you. Therefore, don't make it such a big deal. Keep it in perspective.

> **Student Quote**
>
> "Remember what you have learned about written and oral grammar since elementary school. Those who do will make a great first impression; those who don't will be remembered, but for the wrong reasons."
>
> —*Kristi Geist, management major*

- **Keep breathing.** When you are nervous, you will likely get tight and take short, quick breaths. Take deep breaths, let your shoulders ease down off your neck, and relax.

- **Practice, practice, practice.** The more you practice, the less awkward speaking will feel. And the less awkward you feel, the more natural you will become. You will become somewhat desensitized to this anxiety-provoking experience the more you do it.

THE WHOLE IN ONE

- In today's world, there are many different ways to communicate, making it that much more important that you learn how to communicate effectively.

- Good writing skills are hard to come by and recruiters value them big time. Take advantage of all of the opportunities you have to enhance your writing skills while you are still in school: English and writing courses, writing tutors, and reading, reading, reading.

- Verbal communication is critical in the workplace. Face your public-speaking fears and get out there and practice.

- Take speech communication courses, master your in-class presentations, practice speaking as a leader, and enhance your verbal skills during part-time jobs.

- Make sure to videotape yourself while speaking. It is the best available method of communication training.

BECOME THE BEST YOU...COMMUNICATE EFFECTIVELY!

Chapter 5 Review

Read each question and circle the *best* answer.

1. The author describes a good communicator as one who

   a. is great with his/her language.

   b. is comfortable with his/her language.

   c. speaks well in front of a large group.

   d. speaks well in small-group settings.

2. The most common first impression you give to college and company recruiters is in the form of

   a. a cover letter.

   b. a speech.

   c. a telephone call.

   d. an interview.

3. All of the following are ways to become a better writer except

   a. choosing challenging English teachers.

   b. getting someone to read your writings before submitting them.

   c. using spell-check to correct all of your editing mistakes.

   d. reading a lot in your spare time.

4. *Practicing* is to *baseball* as *reading* is to

   a. writing.

   b. test taking.

   c. watching a play.

   d. job hunting.

5. One of the best ways to train verbal communication is to

   a. talk casually with friends.

   b. use "um" a lot to allow time to think about what to say next.

   c. get plenty of sleep.

   d. videotape yourself giving a speech.

(continued)

(continued)

6. Which of these is not a fact?

a. Public speaking is something feared by many Americans.

b. Most of the time you are your toughest critic.

c. Almost all leaders speak well in front of a group.

d. Practicing your speeches can alleviate awkwardness.

7. In most workplaces, communication skills are utilized

a. daily.

b. every other day.

c. bi-weekly.

d. once a month.

8. Which of these is an opinion?

a. In today's world, there are many different ways to communicate.

b. Verbal communication is critical in most workplaces.

c. Most recruiters value good writing skills.

d. It's difficult to practice communication skills.

9. What is the best summary for this chapter?

a. Students are born with great communication skills, and it is a very difficult skill to improve them.

b. There are many different forms of communication, and it is essential to work on as many as you can to become more credible in the workplace.

c. The most important aspect of communication is writing because every other form of communication stems from writing.

d. There are a lot of different forms of communication, and it is crucial that you work on your speaking skills to better your chances when trying to find a job.

10. What is a synonym for *solicit*?

a. Communicate

b. Talk

c. Write

d. Ask for

6

Career and Character Education Essential #6

Become a Person of Integrity

"When a soldier is given a mission and he responds with 'Roger,' that means he understands the mission and will execute it to the best of his abilities. That one word epitomizes the need for integrity in the military. That soldier's leader has a high degree of assurance that the soldier will perform as expected, and the leader can devote his time to other missions and problems. If he did not believe in the soldier, the leader would have a serious problem."

—Colonel Art Bair (Retired), U.S. Army

How Can I Become a Person of Integrity?

When you hear the term *integrity*, is there somebody who comes to mind? People with integrity are those who are honest, who work hard to be self-sufficient, and who take personal responsibility for their actions. Following, I discuss these underlying qualities that help define a person of strong integrity.

1. Be Honest and Reliable

"Have you heard that the road to ruin is paved with good intentions? Always be asking yourself what is the *right* thing to do. That's what integrity is all about! Ask: 'Does this help me without hurting others?' Most of all, you should be honest to yourself. Anyone can put a spin on a subject or fact to prove whatever they want. Being honest is in the intent and the execution of the intent. The worst thing you can do is make excuses. Be honest and look for the solution!"

—Enterprise Rent-A-Car

The first quality of someone with integrity is honesty. Lately, there have been too many sad displays of the lack of honesty and integrity in the workplace. Because of this, company recruiters often rate honesty/integrity near the top of their wish lists of candidates, as you can see in Appendix A. It's impossible to become the best you when you're not honest and trustworthy. Gaining the trust of your family, friends, teachers, teammates, and coworkers takes a long time, but it can be taken away in a moment. It takes only one dishonest act to lose the trust of others for a very long time, if not forever. Just look at cheating in school. If you see or hear about a student cheating, that label sticks to that student for a very long time, often going on their permanent record. The following are three ways to work on becoming more honest and reliable.

Student Quote

"In a high school setting, it is very easy to conform to the norm in order to feel comfortable in that social setting. However, being honest with yourself and becoming an individual will show far more in any social context than being a cookie-cutter student. Integrity is found through being honest about the person you are and not being afraid to push limits to become the best person that you can be."

—*Jennifer Watkavitch, recent graduate*

Own Up to Your Mistakes

One aspect of being honest, and ultimately a person of integrity, is to take ownership of your actions and admit when you are wrong. Everyone makes mistakes, but too many people want to pass the blame to others. You will gain more respect from people when you step forward and admit that you made a mistake. Think about it. Don't you respect people who take full responsibility for their actions much more than people who pass the blame and get defensive? People with integrity make mistakes just like everybody else, but when they do, they're big enough to own up to them—that's the difference!

"Upon entering the Army, a soldier takes an oath swearing or affirming that '...I will bear true faith and allegiance to the same (the Constitution of the United States)....' Having so sworn, his word becomes his bond; that is, his integrity becomes part of his service. Integrity is important in all aspects of military service because ultimately human life and the future of our country depend on it."

—Colonel Art Bair (Retired), U.S. Army

Follow Through on Your Promises

Company recruiters want to hire graduates who can be relied on to follow through on tasks and to represent their company in a professional and mature way. There is nothing more satisfying for a manager than to delegate a task to a coworker and not have to worry for one second about that coworker getting the task done well and on time. Think about some of your friends or teachers who are always forgetting things. Can you remember a time when you let one of your friends borrow something, and then later found yourself nagging them to give that something back? After a while, you begin to lose trust in your friend. When people are not very reliable, you stop going to them when you need something done. So another aspect of being honest is to work on being reliable.

"It is important for recent graduates to understand that project managers/employers have goals and objectives that they need to achieve. It is through leading that they are able to get these goals achieved. We need employees who can take a list of goals and objectives and go complete them. Project managers do not have the time to continuously 'police' employees on what they have done recently. The project manager needs to know that the employee will complete the tasks presented in a timely fashion. It is also important that employees are motivated to find out what they don't know by being inquisitive and asking questions. However, because time is money, employees/graduates also need to know when to ask questions versus trying to figure it out for themselves."

—PricewaterhouseCoopers

Stop Making So Many Excuses

Do you find yourself telling little white lies or making excuses to your friends and classmates in order to spare their feelings? Many of us hate to disappoint others, so instead of being honest, we make up lame excuses. And that's a third way you can sharpen your honesty: Stop making excuses! Have you ever been on the other end of a lame, made-up excuse? Take a look at a conversation between John and Jacque about going to the movies.

John: Hey Jacque, do you want to go to the movies with us Friday night?

Jacque: I'd love to, but my cousin's coming in from Boston.

John: Bring your cousin along with you!

Jacque: I don't think she's getting in until after dinner.

John: That's okay; we're going to the 9:30 show.

Jacque: Oh, but, um, my cousin's not old enough—she's only 15.

John: That's okay, my mom's going with us.

Jacque: Well, um, I don't think my cousin's much of a movie buff. I wish I could go, but….

John: Well, okay, maybe next time.

Every time you tell a little lie or make a bogus excuse, you're being dishonest and taking a risk that you'll get caught in a lie. In this case, Jacque really just wanted to spend time alone with her cousin whom she hadn't seen for a long while. Would it have been so bad just saying that? Wouldn't it have made Jacque look better if she'd been straight with John? An honest person with integrity is a person who is a straight shooter. How many times have you heard someone say, "Boy that guy doesn't pull any punches. I can always count on him giving me an honest answer. I don't always like what he says, but I sure do respect him for it"? Of course there are times when it's wise to spare others' feelings, but for the most part, be honest with people and avoid making lame excuses!

"Integrity is essential all the time, at day-to-day work, at the water cooler, after hours. Integrity earns you respect. Respect earns you honor, loyalty, and repeat customers."

—Top sales rep Mike Logan (retired), Pfizer

Do What's Right When Nobody Else Is Looking

Having integrity means standing up for what you believe in, regardless of circumstances. One of the most admirable ways to possess integrity is to do good things when nobody else is watching. Try picking up trash during an early morning walk with nobody around or cleaning up around the house without being asked and see how it feels. People with integrity do the right thing for no other reason than that *it's the right thing to do*. Sometimes you do it even though you know it will be difficult or embarrassing. There is no better illustration of this than the following story of a boy and a girl in a third-grade classroom.

In a third-grade classroom, there is a nine-year-old kid sitting at his desk, and all of a sudden there is a puddle between his feet and the front of his pants is wet. He thinks his heart is going to stop because he cannot possibly imagine how this has happened. It's never happened before and he knows that when the boys find out he will never hear the end of it. When the girls find out, they'll never speak to him again as long as he lives.

The boy believes his heart is going to stop; he puts his head down and prays, "Dear God, this is an emergency! I need help now! Five minutes from now I'm dead meat." He looks up from his prayer, and here comes the teacher with a look in her eyes that says he has been discovered.

As the teacher is walking toward him, a classmate named Susie is carrying a gold-fish bowl that is filled with water. Susie trips in front of the teacher and inexplicably dumps the bowl of water in the boy's lap. The boy pretends to be angry, but all the while is saying to himself, "Thank you, Lord! Thank you, Lord!" Now all of a sudden, instead of being the object of ridicule, the boy is the object of sympathy.

The teacher rushes him downstairs and gives him gym shorts to put on while his pants dry out. All the other children are on their hands and knees cleaning up around his desk. The sympathy is wonderful. But as life would have it, the ridicule that should have been his has been transferred to someone else—Susie. She tries to help, but they tell her to get out. "You've done enough, you klutz!"

(continued)

(continued)

> Finally, at the end of the day, as they are waiting for the bus, the boy walks over to Susie and whispers, "You did that on purpose, didn't you?" Susie whispers back, "I wet my pants once, too."
>
> —Anonymous

2. Be Self-Sufficient and Take Personal Responsibility

"Self-sufficiency benefits our company because the people we hire are capable of making ideas happen. Our collaborative environment encourages people to show their initiative, share their perspectives, and contribute to client successes. Self-sufficient individuals also take ownership over their careers and satisfaction, which benefits both the individuals and also our company."

—Accenture

People with integrity have pride in themselves and their work. They work hard and find a way to get things done without relying too much on others. Today, it is more important than ever to be self-sufficient. It is projected that you will most likely change jobs between 10 and 15 times in a lifetime, while changing entire career fields three to five times. When it comes to changing jobs, do you really think your old company will help you get a job with a different one? Of course not. You'll need to be self-sufficient and take control of your own career!

Don't look for people to do things for you, like helping you write a paper or changing your car tire. Think about the adage, "Give a man a fish and he'll eat for a day. Teach a man to fish and he'll eat for a lifetime." You want to learn how to do things yourself so you will be able to do them throughout your life and teach others along the way.

Company recruiters like to hire self-sufficient graduates. However, what does that really mean? How do you become self-sufficient? You don't just wake up one day being self-sufficient. The key to becoming self-sufficient is to identify the underlying qualities that enable you to be self-sufficient and more responsible. Following are three essential qualities of a responsible, self-sufficient person.

Be a Critical Thinker

The first quality of a responsible, self-sufficient person is the ability to think for yourself and analyze situations. As you are tested and face new challenges in school and in life, you cannot always count on your teachers, counselors, or parents for the answers. It is impossible to become self-sufficient if you do not begin to challenge yourself and use your mind to think critically about issues. You must have enough self-confidence to analyze issues and problems and work things out on your own.

If you want to develop your analytical skills, make sure to take your share of math classes. Most schools require that you take a certain number of courses in math, but most students do little more than the minimum. Many students believe that math is a waste of time. People always ask, "Why do we have to do math? We're never going to use this in life." Well, maybe you won't be solving complex mathematical equations on your job, but you will be forced to think critically, analyze problems, and come up with your own solutions.

My sister, a high school math teacher, uses the following explanation when her students ask, "Why do we have to learn this stuff? We'll never use it in the future."

> During practice, do football players do push-ups and sit-ups? Sure. But wait, I've gone to a lot of football games, and I've never seen the football players out on the field actually doing push-ups and sit-ups during the game. So why do they waste the time doing push-ups and sit-ups in practice if they never do push-ups and sit-ups during the game?
>
> Just like push-ups and sit-ups help make football players stronger—which indirectly makes them better football players during the game—doing math and solving mathematical problems helps to strengthen your mind and make you better equipped to think critically and solve problems that you will encounter throughout your life.

In addition to taking math courses, take the time necessary to reflect critically on situations and issues that you face and to formulate your own thoughts and solutions. You will frequently come across issues and problems in class, during your part-time job, in extracurricular activities, and with your friends. The more you get involved—in and out of class—the more you will practice using your analytical skills, and thus the more self-sufficient you will

Student Quote

"Character is an important and necessary quality to have if you want to market to both colleges and companies alike. In a college or job interview, you want to be able to stand out from the crowd and show that you are an individual who has her own set of values, skills, and abilities that differ and exceed your competition."

—Kim Brown, recent graduate

become. Challenge yourself to think critically on your own, formulate solutions, and stand by your position in a firm, yet tactful, way.

Show Initiative

A second quality of a responsible, self-sufficient person is being a self-starter. In today's workplace, companies are forced to be more productive with fewer people. In the 1980s and 1990s, this work trend was referred to as downsizing or rightsizing. Companies do not have the time to take new employees by the hand and help them figure out everything. They are looking for graduates who are self-starters. Companies do not want to have to tell their employees to do everything; they want their employees to seek out or initiate work to be done. If there is a better way of doing things, they want their employees to have enough initiative to bring it to their attention.

The best way to learn how to take initiative is to find something you love or believe in and take responsibility for making it better. Join that club or organization that excites you and think of new programs or services to offer. Sometimes you do not have to create new programs, but initiate ways to improve existing ones. Get involved in your community and volunteer your time. Community service agencies are always looking for energetic volunteers to come in and start new programs for the people that they serve. Get involved in your student government and initiate change and new ideas. Taking on a leadership role in school is a prime way to develop and ultimately demonstrate your initiative. There are countless ways to develop your initiative—just look around you, choose something you are passionate about, and make a difference.

Student Quote

"Honesty and integrity at the high school level are truly essential to being a good person and being successful. Being honest with someone does not mean telling them how you feel without regard for how you tell them. Disagreements happen and sometimes they are unavoidable, but if we are honest with them in a tactful way, our integrity will not suffer a loss. When we lose our integrity through a lack of honesty, we have lost two things that are extremely hard to earn again."

—Ellery Loomis,
recent graduate

"Many years ago, an Enterprise employee in Florida decided that it would be a good business decision to pick up his customers at their home or office and bring them to the Enterprise branch. He implemented the policy in his branch and began to tell his colleagues about this practice. This idea became more and more popular throughout the company as others saw what a benefit it was to the company's customers, and eventually this practice became implemented company-wide. Because of his initiative and his willingness to take a chance, Enterprise is now known as the company that will 'Pick You Up.'"

—Enterprise Rent-A-Car

Be Resourceful

A third key to becoming more responsible and self-sufficient is being resourceful. Have you ever heard someone say, "She's so resourceful"? Did you ever stop and think what that means? When someone is resourceful, it means that they have the knowledge, imagination, skills, contacts, and assertiveness necessary to get things done or figure things out efficiently. Look at the following scenario that effectively illustrates resourcefulness.

CASE IN POINT: TWO RESOURCEFUL CLASSMATES

Todd and Tracy, two high school classmates, volunteer in their community. They go twice a week to a children's agency that works with disadvantaged youth. The head of the agency mentioned to Todd and Tracy that she wished the agency had the funds to purchase computers for the kids. Todd and Tracy began exploring ways to get computers for the kids. They went to their local community college and met with the head of the computer department. They asked if the department head knew any technology companies in the area that would be willing to hand down older computers. He came up with a list of seven companies.

Todd and Tracy called each company and scheduled a meeting with their respective public relations directors. They knew that public relations divisions focus on maintaining a good, positive image with the public and surrounding community. During the meetings, Todd and Tracy informed the directors of the computer needs of the children, and also said that they were planning on approaching every computer company in the community to donate old computers. In addition, they mentioned that the local newspaper reporters were going to write a big article in the newspaper, highlighting the generosity of these participating companies. After meeting with the seven companies, they were able to get computers from three of the seven companies. The head of the agency was thrilled. She could not believe how resourceful Todd and Tracy were.

Todd and Tracy were indeed resourceful. They used their contacts and resources in their community to obtain a list of companies. They also met with the editor-in-chief of the local newspaper and asked her to write a feature article. Todd and Tracy knew that this would encourage the public relations directors to help, because it would be good publicity for the companies. They were assertive in contacting and scheduling meetings with the directors and in selling them on the importance of participating.

"Accenture seeks students who possess demonstrated leadership qualities and self-sufficiency, among other attributes. We believe these qualities are important because if graduates demonstrate that they are confident and resourceful, it may be easier for them to integrate, contribute, and start to have an impact from the very beginning of their careers."

—Accenture

Becoming resourceful is similar to developing initiative. You have to get involved in school and in your community. The more active you become within organizations, the more people and contacts you'll meet and the more knowledge you will gain. As you become active in community service, you will be forced to be more resourceful because there is often little money and few resources with which to work.

Join student chapters of associations and attend conferences. For example, some Rotary clubs (consisting of business leaders in the community) have a student chapter called Rotaract. High school and college students can join Rotaract and get involved in leadership, professional development, and community service through this organization. The students also get to meet and mingle with their sponsoring Rotary members. Another way to gain contacts and become more resourceful is to participate in any career-mentoring program that your school sponsors. Sign up, get matched with a professional mentor in a career field of interest, and start networking.

Spending time as an intern or part-time worker at a professional organization is another great way to become more resourceful and self-sufficient. Seeking out and completing an internship or an apprenticeship will allow you to experience firsthand what it is like to work in a professional environment. You know how a lot of teachers and other adults like to say, "Wait until you're in the real world—it's not like school." Well, even though you may get sick of hearing that, the statement does have some truth to it. While you are soaking in the environment and learning firsthand from those on the job, you will automatically become more resourceful.

In summary, becoming a person of integrity takes hard work, pride, perseverance, self-confidence, honesty, and personal responsibility. What will it take for you to be known as "a person with a lot of integrity"?

THE WHOLE IN ONE

- A person of integrity is a person who is honest and responsible.
- It's important to own up to your mistakes, follow through on your promises, and stop making so many excuses!
- Companies and organizations today don't have the time to take you by the hand and teach you everything. You must become self-sufficient.
- Self-sufficient, responsible people are critical thinkers, self-starters, and resourceful. The key to developing one's self-sufficiency is to get out there and get involved.

BECOME THE BEST YOU...BECOME A PERSON OF INTEGRITY!

Chapter 6 Review

Read each question and circle the *best* answer.

1. **When you make a mistake, it is best to**

   a. own up to it.

   b. lie about it.

   c. accept it but don't let anyone else know.

   d. tell someone so you feel better.

2. **When a person does not want to do something, it is better to**

   a. lie and please someone.

   b. tell the truth and probably disappoint someone.

   c. tell the truth with tact and hope the person understands.

   d. tell a lie and disappoint someone.

3. **The author's purpose for using the analogy of football players doing sit-ups and push-ups to students learning is to show students that**

   a. they need to learn a lot of skills in school and have to enjoy learning them.

   b. the process of learning helps them expand their minds and be better problem solvers.

   c. learning skills in school directly enhances their chances of getting a job.

   d. they should try to learn everything because they don't know what their future jobs will entail.

4. **A great way to learn how to take initiative and be a self-starter is to**

   a. join a club with your friends and communicate with them often.

   b. join a club and try to change everything about the club.

   c. join a club you are passionate about and try to make it better.

   d. join a club you don't know much about and learn everything you can about it.

5. **All of these are qualities of a resourceful person except being**

   a. extremely intelligent.

   b. knowledgeable.

   c. analytical.

   d. assertive.

6. **The moral of the "wet pants" story is**
   a. take the blame always.
   b. always do what's right.
   c. don't be so selfish.
   d. jump in and take initiative.

7. **Managers love it when you follow through on your promises because**
   a. they don't have to do any work.
   b. they'll look good in turn to their bosses.
   c. they don't have to repeat things.
   d. they have peace of mind because they know you'll come through.

8. **Honesty and integrity have become more important lately because**
   a. of people lying on their resumes.
   b. honesty is the cornerstone of all relationships.
   c. of all the recent company examples of lack of integrity in the world of work.
   d. of the increased amount of cheating in the schools.

9. **All of these are characteristics of an honest and reliable person except**
   a. resolving conflicts efficiently.
   b. owning your mistakes.
   c. following through on promises.
   d. avoiding excuses.

10. **In today's business environment, employers prefer workers who**
    a. follow directions carefully.
    b. just do what they are told.
    c. are self-starters.
    d. maintain the status quo.

Career and Character Education
Essential #7

Pay Attention to the Right Things

"A leader certainly must be able to see the big picture, but also be grounded enough to recognize how to get from point A to point B (in other words, the street smarts to not only know what will work, but also to infuse a dose of reality into the process or outcome). To realistically demonstrate these skills requires experience. With more experience, the ability to see the big picture becomes more pronounced, as does the street smarts to really know all the angles and what really works."

—Smart and Associates, LLP

The Importance of Paying Attention to the Right Things

Have you ever found yourself daydreaming in class and not paying attention to the teacher? Who hasn't, right? And then you finally "woke up" from your daydream and thought to yourself, "Oh wow—I haven't listened to one thing the teacher said for the last 10 minutes. I'll have to get the notes from somebody to fill in what I missed." Or maybe you remember a time you were walking down the hall talking to a friend about something exciting, and you ran into somebody coming the other way. The person you ran into likely said, "Hey, pay attention to where you're going!" Or when you were supposed to "keep an eye" on your little brother or sister, and just when you forgot to do your job for a few seconds, he or she fell down and your mom yelled out, "Hey, I told you to watch out for your sister/ brother!" Well, it's pretty safe to say that, during those times, you weren't paying attention to the right thing at the right time.

You're probably saying to yourself, "Yeah, so what—what's the big deal?" Not paying attention to the right things at the right time actually *wasn't* too big a deal in the three examples presented above. But what if you were a security guard at a bank, and you were so intent on checking the scores of last night's game in the newspaper that you didn't notice two guys with ski masks coming inside until it was too late to do anything about it? Or what if you're a bus driver, and you become so focused on fixing the radio that you didn't see the sharp turn ahead?

Paying attention to the right things at the right time does matter—sometimes a lot more than other times! And to perform well and be successful in school, on the job, and in life, paying attention to the right things at the right time is half the battle! In this chapter, you will learn how to shift your attention to fit the situation you are in, which in turn will enable you to enhance your performance in everything you do!

The Three Attentional Channels

There are three primary "Attentional Channels"—*Aware, Conceptual, and Focused*—and every person has a tendency to favor one of them.*

This model of attention was introduced by Robert Nideffer in 1974 and formed the basis for his psychological inventory, The Attentional & Interpersonal Style (TAIS) inventory. It has been extended and refined into Attention Control Training mental preparation programs in all arenas by Nideffer and Robin W. Pratt.

Some people spend most of the time paying attention to what's going on around them. These people have a high level of *awareness* and are therefore mostly "on the Aware Channel." Other people spend most of their time paying attention to big-picture concepts "in their head" while deeply analyzing things. These people are highly *conceptual* and therefore are mostly "on the Conceptual Channel." Finally, there are people who spend most of their time paying close attention to one thing at a time. These people are highly *focused* and therefore are mostly "on the Focused Channel." You see, if you can identify the Attentional Channel that you're on most of the time, as well as the one you're hardly ever on, it will help you to figure out why you're not performing as well as you could in certain situations in school, at home, or when you're with friends. We'll break down the three Attentional Channels, and then you can begin identifying which channel *you* tend to be on most of the time.

The Aware Channel

People who are more *aware* always seem to have a good sense of what's going on around them. Sometimes it's referred to as good *street sense*. A strong Aware person can smell trouble a mile away and can sense when someone is down and needs a lift. They tend to pay more attention to the external world around them than they do processing big ideas in their head or narrowly focusing in on one thing.

There are many examples of when it's important to be "on the Aware Channel." We already saw through the preceding examples how important it is for a security guard and bus driver to be on their Aware Channels! Another good example of when it's important is a teacher out at recess. If the teacher is focused on one child, let's say helping to tie his shoes, or daydreaming about the upcoming weekend, she/he may miss one of the children running across the street chasing a kickball or two kids slugging away at each other in a fight. For teachers to be effective while monitoring recess and perform well at that time and place, it is critical that their attention is centered on being *aware* of their surroundings! Paying attention to the right things at the right times, then, really can have a huge impact! In this case, being on the Aware Channel out at recess has a great impact on a teacher's success.

> ### *Student Quote*
>
> "Understanding your surroundings will serve you for the rest of your life. This includes being able to recognize and understand that your success in a group hinges upon the ability of the group to see what is working and what needs some extra attention. This includes being able to recognize that every person has strengths and that utilizing those strengths is the most effective way to succeed."
>
> —*Ellery Loomis, recent graduate*

Reflecting on How Aware *You* Are

Is the Aware Channel a channel that you tend to be on most of the time? Do people who know you well frequently tell you that you're perceptive? Do you find it hard to stay focused on reading or writing in class because of distractions around you? Are you one of the first ones to notice when something's wrong with a friend, classmate, or teammate? These are the types of questions you should ponder in determining your level of awareness.

EXERCISE

To begin identifying your level of awareness, answer the following questions by circling the number that best applies to you:**

1 = Strongly Disagree

2 = Disagree

3 = Agree

4 = Strongly Agree

1. My friends and family tell me that I'm very perceptive.   1   2   3   4

2. When something's wrong or somebody's in trouble, I'm one of the first ones to notice or sense it.   1   2   3   4

3. In class, I get distracted easily when somebody gets up or when somebody else walks by the door in the hallway.   1   2   3   4

4. I can easily tell when others are talking about me.   1   2   3   4

5. When I'm at the mall, I spend a lot of time observing other people and soaking in the environment.   1   2   3   4

6. When I'm at a party, it's hard for me to stay focused listening to one person because of all the other people around.   1   2   3   4

TOTAL AWARE SCORE (Add up the numbers across all six questions): _____

NOTE: We'll use this total score later to help determine your Attentional Profile.

***This exercise is an approximation of the attentional part of the extended psychological inventory, The Attentional & Interpersonal Style (TAIS) inventory, developed by Robert M. Nideffer, founder of Enhanced Performance Systems (EPS). For more information on this instrument and its uses, see www.enhanced-performance.com. The following questions were constructed by the current author, Bob Orndorff, who has been certified in the use of TAIS inventory by EPS.*

The Conceptual Channel

The second Attentional Channel is the Conceptual Channel. People who are *conceptual* are usually described as "daydreamers" who tend to process things deeply and analyze things to death.

One of the most important times to be on the Conceptual Channel is when making decisions in life. When making decisions, it is critical to step back, analyze all the options, and think through the various consequences. One of the most important decisions you'll need to make in life is what kind of career you'd like to have. When choosing a career, it is critical to thoroughly analyze career options of interest and to weigh out the pros and cons.

Another situation when it's important to be conceptual is when you're taking on a leadership role. Leaders— whether in school, at work, or in the community—need to be conceptual as they strategically plan out their vision for where they want their group/team to go in the future. Leaders can't just focus in on one thing; they need to see the big picture and how all the little pieces fit together!

A third situation where the Conceptual Channel comes in extremely handy is reflecting on your actions and behaviors. The only real way we can change and develop and ultimately become a better person is to reflect openly and honestly on our actions and behaviors. When you make a mistake or upset a friend or family member, you should spend time analyzing what you did and figure out the best way to make things right. How many times have you heard your parents or teachers say, "Learn from your mistakes"? Well, the only way you can learn from your mistakes is to analyze what you did wrong so you won't do it again! Note that when you succeed at something and do things well, it's just as important to take time to reflect on what you did well

Student Quote

"Creating the vision of our group is fun, but when the high school year is half over do we all have the same level of enthusiasm? By constantly setting short-term goals that align with our group's long-term goals, we can maintain that level of enthusiasm. Every little accomplishment should be documented and celebrated because we as a group have accomplished these items and we are keeping the big picture in mind."

—*Ellery Loomis,*
recent graduate

and why you were able to succeed. Doing this will enable you to take what you did well to future similar situations.

Thus, in order to make good decisions, perform well as a leader, and reflect on your actions and behaviors, it's important to be on the Conceptual Channel!

Reflecting on How Conceptual *You* Are

How conceptual are you? Are you conceptual when you need to be? Do you find yourself daydreaming a lot? Are people too frequently asking you, "Hello, are you in there?" Are you a deep thinker? Have you been told that you over-analyze things too much? These are the types of questions you should consider in determining how conceptual you are.

EXERCISE

To begin identifying how conceptual you are, answer the following questions by circling the number that best applies to you:

1 = Strongly Disagree

2 = Disagree

3 = Agree

4 = Strongly Agree

1. I daydream a lot—my head is always "in the clouds."	1	2	3	4
2. I over-analyze decisions and other things.	1	2	3	4
3. I'm a deep thinker and analyze key issues in our world.	1	2	3	4
4. I analyze myself a lot: what I did well and what I did poorly.	1	2	3	4
5. I usually want to know *why* things are done a certain way.	1	2	3	4
6. I tend to look at the big picture—not all the details.	1	2	3	4

TOTAL CONCEPTUAL SCORE (Add the numbers for all six questions): _____

NOTE: We'll use this total score later to help determine your Attentional Profile.

The Focused Channel

The third and final Attentional Channel is the Focused Channel. People who are focused are able to concentrate on one thing at a time and get a lot done. They pay attention to details and follow through on what they said they would do. There are many professions where it is critical to be on the Focused Channel. When a surgeon loses focus or an airplane inspector fails to check all the details, people lose their lives! If a psychologist begins daydreaming while his or her client is talking, critical information may be missed. In everyday life, being on the Focused Channel is essential to being a strong listener. As we saw in Chapter 1, being a good listener and developing positive relationships in your life are important qualities in a people person. When a friend is trying to tell you something important in the hallway, and you get distracted by people walking by (Aware Channel), or you're off in your head thinking about a previous concern (Conceptual Channel), you're not being a very good friend because you failed to be on the right channel (Focused Channel) at the right time!

"I would suggest that the most appropriate channel for a person starting their career is the Focus capacity. Again, going back to leadership, it is critical to take ownership and carry an event through to completion, which includes attending to all the details and keeping your eye on the desired outcome at the same time. We would place new hires in a role that enables them to demonstrate this competency, or Focus, by keeping roles and assignments well defined and as narrow as possible. Over time, as they mature and successfully demonstrate the appropriate competencies, we gradually increase their scope of responsibility, thus increasing their need to see a bigger picture and providing them with the appropriate 'street smarts' to be effective."

—Smart and Associates, LLP

To be successful academically, being on the Focused Channel is necessary in most situations. Staying focused in class and concentrating on what your teachers are saying has a big effect on your understanding of the subject matter. In those classes where the subject is boring to you, it's very easy to daydream because almost everything else you think about is more interesting and exciting than what's being taught. These are the times that you need to work the hardest at staying on the Focused Channel! Another common challenge that students face is staying focused on reading assignments. When you allow yourself to get on the Aware and Conceptual Channels, doesn't it take you forever to get through a chapter?

> *Student Quote*
>
> "Being focused is one of the hardest things to do in high school and even harder in college. There is so much going on with school work, family, friends, clubs, and your job that focusing on one thing at a time seems impossible at times. Time management is very important. Start making lists, prioritizing everything you need to do in a given day."
>
> —*Michelle Kelly, education major*

Reflecting on How Focused *You* Are

Once again, it's important to determine how focused you tend to be, and if you're focused when you need to be. Are you task-oriented? Are you able to get a lot of things done in a short period of time? Are you able to concentrate on what you're doing? Do you tend to the details when you're planning a trip? Are you a good listener? These are the types of questions you should consider in determining how focused you are.

EXERCISE

To begin identifying how focused you are, answer the following questions by circling the number that best applies to you:

1 = Strongly Disagree

2 = Disagree

3 = Agree

4 = Strongly Agree

1. I'm able to pay close attention to my teachers in class.	1 2 3 4
2. I listen closely to friends, classmates, and family.	1 2 3 4
3. I'm able to complete a task without getting distracted.	1 2 3 4
4. I'm a "doer"—I get a lot done in a short period of time.	1 2 3 4
5. I don't have much trouble staying focused on what I'm reading.	1 2 3 4
6. I tend to think through the details of what needs to be done.	1 2 3 4

TOTAL FOCUSED SCORE (Add up the numbers across all six questions): _____

NOTE: Next, we'll use this total score to help determine your Attentional Profile.

Your Attentional Profile

Now that you have a better understanding of the three Attentional Channels, it's important to identify which channel is most prevalent for you and which channel is least prevalent for you. In doing this, you will be establishing your *Attentional Profile*. An Attentional Profile is simply a rank order of the three Attentional Channels. For example, if Joe's most prevalent channel is Conceptual, and his least prevalent is Focused, Joe's Attentional Profile is Conceptual, Aware, Focused. This profile reminds Joe that he tends to be most frequently on the Conceptual Channel, somewhere off in his head, and that he will need to work hard at getting on the Focused Channel at times when he needs to be more focused.

At this point, the best educated guess to figuring out your Attentional Profile is to add up the total for each exercise, and place the highest score first, the next highest second, and the least highest third. For example, if you score 9 on Aware, 20 on Conceptual, and 15 on Focused, your Attentional Profile would be Conceptual, Focused, Aware.

My Attentional Profile

Total Aware Score: _____

Total Conceptual Score: _____

Total Focused Score: _____

Thus, my Attentional Profile is _____ _____ _____

(**NOTE:** See your teacher or school counselor to inquire about completing the Attentional Survey to receive more precise scores and a more accurate Attentional Profile.)

No One Attentional Profile Is Better than Another

You may wonder whether your Attentional Profile is good or bad. It's like playing "Rock, Paper, Scissors." For those of you who have never played, on the count of three, two people make the shape of a rock, paper, or scissors with their hand. The winner is determined as follows:

If one picks Paper, and the other picks Rock, the Paper covers the Rock, so Paper wins.

If one picks Paper, and the other picks Scissors, the Scissors cut the Paper, so Scissors wins.

If one picks Rock, and the other picks Scissors, the Rock breaks the Scissors, so Rock wins.

So, as you see, out of the three choices (Rock, Paper, Scissors), there's no one that's better than the other. *It depends on the situation!* In the situation where your opponent picks paper, it would be best if you pick scissors. In the situation where your opponent picks scissors, it would be best if you pick rock. Likewise, in the situation where a friend needs you to listen to them, it's best if your Attentional Profile begins with Focused. In the situation where you're asked to watch over some children, it's best if Aware is the strongest channel within your Attentional Profile.

Student Quote

"It is important to have all of these types of Attentional Channels because they differ in importance from situation to situation. You could be asked on a history test, "What fueled the hostilities at the beginning of World War II?" This question asks the student to analyze the whole concept (Conceptual). There could also be a question asking what day the Nazis surrendered, which would be a question that would pertain to details (Focused). Both of these types of Attentional Channels are important to full understanding."

—Kim Brown,
recent graduate

However, even when your Attentional Profile doesn't fit a particular situation, you can still make adjustments to get on the right Attentional Channel. Knowing your Attentional Profile (where you're most likely to pay attention) can help you to make the right adjustments to your everyday behaviors and actions and ultimately perform better in and out of class.

Adjusting Your Attentional Channels to Perform Better in Life

So what's the point to all of this "Attentional" stuff? How can you use Attentional Channels to become the best you? Following is the key to applying the Attentional Channels to your life and becoming a better you.

> To become a better student, a better athlete, a better friend, a better worker, or an overall better person, you must identify situations in your life when you need to be more Aware, more Conceptual, and more Focused, and make adjustments to your normal way of doing things to get on the right channel!

You see, if you just allow your natural Attentional Profile to take over, sometimes it will work, and sometimes it won't. For example, if your Attentional Profile is Focused, Aware, Conceptual, and you don't make any *deliberate* adjustments, you'll perform well in life's situations that require a strong focus, such as reading and listening to someone; however, you won't perform so well in situations that require conceptual attention, such as designing a plan and analyzing your mistakes. There are two steps to complete in utilizing the Attentional Channels and performing better in life.

Step 1: Identify Situations When You Need to Be More Aware, Conceptual, or Focused

Following is a worksheet that will enable you to begin identifying key situations in your life when you need to be more Aware, Conceptual, or Focused.

Your Attentional Worksheet***

Aware

What do I need to be aware of in school, at home, and in other parts of my life?

_____

_____

_____

When am I oblivious to my surroundings?

_____

_____

_____

When am I sensitive to and closely reading my environment?

_____

_____

_____

_____

Conceptual

What's important for me to analyze or consider in school, at home, and in other situations?

_____

_____

_____

_____

(continued)

***Adapted from the "Attentional Worksheet" in the workbook Paying Attention to the Right Things: A Leaders' Guide to Professional Development and Staying on Track *by Dr. Robin Pratt, President, Enhanced Performance Services.*

(continued)

When do I tend to NOT analyze or reflect on things?

_____

_____

_____

_____

When am I thinking, planning, analyzing, or anticipating consequences?

_____

_____

_____

_____

Focused

What do I need to stay focused on in school, at home, and in other situations?

_____

_____

_____

_____

When am I inattentive with a short attention span?

_____

_____

_____

_____

When am I focused and attending to the details?

_____

_____

_____

_____

Talk to Your Significant Others to Identify Key Situations in Your Life

In addition to completing this worksheet, you should talk with various family members, friends, teachers, counselors, and other people who know you well. These significant people in your life can further help you identify important situations that are both consistent and inconsistent with your natural Attentional Profile.

Step 2: Make Adjustments Before, During, and After These Key Situations

Next you need to make adjustments, and there are three times you can do this.

Make Adjustments Before Situations

After you identify the key situations in your life, you must then think of ways to increase the chances of being on the right channel when these situations occur in the future. For example, if you're having trouble focusing on your homework assignments (because Focused is last on your Attentional Profile), maybe there are changes you can make ahead of time to eliminate the distractions. Obvious changes would be closing your door, turning off music, or asking your family members to take phone messages when friends call.

Make Adjustments During Situations

Sometimes making adjustments is as easy as being conscious of your Attentional Profile and catching yourself drifting away from your weakest channel towards your strongest. The following example helps illustrate this point.

JOE LISTENER

Joe has always had a tough time listening to people, especially when he's in a large group setting. Joe's Attentional Profile is Aware, Conceptual, Focused. Thus, in a large group or social gathering, Joe's natural tendency is to pay more attention to people around him than on listening to one person. Typically, while Joe is talking to somebody, he begins on the Focused Channel (his weakest channel), but he easily gets distracted by other people around him and drifts to the Aware Channel—his strongest channel.

(continued)

(continued)

Joe recently became aware of his Attentional Profile, and realized that he tends to lose focus when listening to people. At the next high school dance, Joe made a conscious effort to stay focused on the people he was talking to rather than drift away and scope the crowd. Joe caught himself slipping away to his Awareness Channel a few times, but he quickly recovered and switched back to the Focused Channel. Joe felt a lot better about himself afterwards. It felt good really listening to his friends. To this day, Joe continues to have to remind himself of his tendency to drift, but because he's been working on it for over a year now, he's forming better habits of listening attentively for longer periods of time.

Make Adjustments After Situations

After these key situations take place, it's important to reflect on how well you performed. If you performed well, try to determine why it went so well. What Attentional Channel(s) did you utilize the most, and when did you utilize them? Conversely, if you performed poorly, try to determine what went wrong. Were you on the wrong Attentional Channel most of the time? Which Attentional Channel should have been utilized more?

To change and become a better person, it's necessary to go against your natural tendencies at times. When it comes to paying attention, it's necessary to go against your natural Attentional Profile at times to perform better in certain situations. You can do it!

You now have the knowledge necessary to identify situations in which you want to perform better and to make the appropriate adjustments. So get out there and pay attention to the right things at the right time and become the best you!

Student Quote

"You are not going to succeed in life if you are a great thinker (Conceptual), but you cannot communicate your ideas and interact with people (Aware). Likewise, it will not be very beneficial if you can talk to people, but you do not know what you are talking about. It is the people who can integrate these attributes who find success in life."

—*Brian Jacobs, political science major*

THE WHOLE IN ONE

- Paying attention to the right things at the right time is a key to performing well in life.
- There are three primary Attentional Channels (where you're paying attention): Aware, Conceptual, and Focused.
  - The Aware Channel enables people to be street smart, always perceptive to their surroundings.
  - The Conceptual Channel causes people to be daydreaming, analyzing, and thinking deeply about big-picture issues.
  - The Focused Channel enables people to attend to details and concentrate on one thing for longer periods of time.
- An Attentional Profile is the rank-order of the three Attentional Channels, from strongest to weakest.
- The key to utilizing the Attentional Channels is first identifying situations where you need to be more Aware, Conceptual, and Focused, and then making adjustments to your natural Attentional Profile to force yourself to stay on the right channel at the right time.

BECOME THE BEST YOU...PAY ATTENTION TO THE RIGHT THINGS!

Chapter 7 Review

Read each question and circle the *best* answer.

1. **This chapter was written to explain to students that they should pay attention**

   a. all of the time.

   b. some of the time.

   c. to the right things at the right time.

   d. all of the above.

2. **Which one of these is not an Attention Channel?**

   a. Aware

   b. Thinking

   c. Conceptual

   d. Focused

3. **Someone who is said to have "street sense" is**

   a. aware.

   b. knowledgeable.

   c. conscious of highway safety.

   d. conceptual.

4. **When performing brain surgery, a doctor should stay on the _____ Channel.**

   a. Focused

   b. Conceptual

   c. Aware

   d. All of the above

5. **People who process thoughts deeply and analyze things to death are**

   a. Conceptual.

   b. day-dreamers.

   c. Focused.

   d. Aware.

6. **The only real way you can change and ultimately become a better person is to**

   a. ask your best friend about your strengths and weaknesses.

   b. ask your parents about their backgrounds.

   c. join as many activities as possible.

   d. reflect on your own actions openly and honestly.

7. **Being on the Focused Channel can help you with what very important inter-personal trait?**

   a. Speaking

   b. Listening

   c. Communicating

   d. Reflecting

8. **In the sentence, "It's important to identify which channel is most prevalent for you," *prevalent* means**

   a. common.

   b. important.

   c. stressful.

   d. embarrassing.

9. **It is crucial to make adjustments _____ key situations in your life.**

   a. before

   b. during

   c. after

   d. all of the above

10. **The best statement to sum up this chapter would be:**

    a. Pay attention all of the time.

    b. Pay attention to the things that can benefit you now.

    c. Pay attention to the future.

    d. Pay attention to the right things at the right time.

*Career and Character Education
Essential #8*

Become a Leader

"In talking about teamwork, Microsoft CEO Steve Ballmer once said, 'At the end of every day, I'd like people to go home asking: Did I make the people around me more productive? Did I help them get more done? Did I offer insights that will enable them to do their job better?' Microsoft calls teamwork 'making others great.' This means problem solving and collaboration at the individual level and focusing on being good managers and leaders through strong hiring, management, communication, and motivation of teams."

—Microsoft

Why Is It Important to Become a Leader?

When you take on a leadership role, you develop a long list of skills and qualities that colleges and companies are looking for in graduates. Not only is it important to show college and company recruiters that you have the ability to lead, but being a leader is also one of the best ways of appreciating the essence of teamwork. In addition, whether you are in a leadership role or not, there are many leadership qualities and skills that are great to have in life as well as at work—skills that go a long way in helping you become the best you. Here are some of the key skills and qualities that are developed during leadership experiences:

- Initiative
- Self-confidence
- Organizational skills
- Teamwork
- Conflict resolution
- Time management
- Strategic planning
- Program coordination/event planning

It is important for you to explore opportunities where you can serve as a leader in order to gain these valuable skills.

Student Quote

"Leadership isn't limited to being president of a club or organization. Leadership is defined by being the best at what you do and putting forth the best effort that you can give. As you challenge yourself to be a leader and not a follower, not only will you define your own character traits and learn about yourself as a person, but you will inspire others to push their own limits and better themselves as well."

—*Jennifer Watkavitch, recent graduate*

"Leadership can be defined many different ways. In our case, we certainly look for and value leadership skills in our people. From the staff level to the partner level, each person must be able to demonstrate core leadership characteristics such as setting the appropriate strategy/direction to complete the task at hand, taking ownership for particular results, and taking whatever measures necessary to achieve results."

—Smart and Associates

How Do You Become a Leader?

To become a leader, you don't just wake up one day and say, "I'm going to be a leader," and then figure out what group you plan on leading. The best way to become a leader is to start by finding a club, team, or group about which you're passionate. After you're in a group that you like, you'll naturally want to get more involved and ultimately take on more and more responsibility. And then one day, you *will* wake up and find yourself in a leadership role—but it won't happen overnight! Following is a good illustration of how you can become a leader.

THE CASE OF STEPHANIE

Stephanie was a sophomore in high school. She had always been interested in learning about different countries and cultures. Her family had done a lot of traveling, visiting more than 10 countries since Stephanie was in first grade. Stephanie wanted to get more involved in high school and found out about the International Affairs Club (IAC). She joined the club and went to all the meetings. During one of the meetings in the spring, the president announced that the IAC was going to be active in helping an exchange student from Australia feel more welcomed when he arrived in the fall. The president asked for volunteers to join a Welcoming Committee, and Stephanie enthusiastically offered her assistance. Throughout the spring, Stephanie was the most active of her committee members and came up with many creative ways to smooth the transition for the exchange student.

Right before the summer, the IAC met to elect officers for the following year. Because Stephanie did such a great job on the Welcoming Committee, she was nominated for the vice president position and received enough votes to win! During her junior year, Stephanie took on more and more responsibility as vice president of the IAC and was thought of highly among the club's members. At the end of her junior year, Stephanie was nominated for president and unanimously was voted in! Looking back, Stephanie's experience as president of the IAC was her most rewarding and valuable experience. And it all started from joining a club that fit her passion!

There are a lot of clubs, teams, and groups in high school. I'm sure you can think of one that you'd be excited to join! Take that first step in joining a club and becoming active. Keep your eyes open for leadership opportunities. And remember, you don't need to become president to have a strong leadership experience. You can develop your leadership skills by heading up even a small committee or project within the group you join. The important thing is to find your passion and get involved, and then good things will happen!

Where Do You Become a Leader?

There are many ways and places to become a leader. You can become a leader in school, at work, in the community, or on athletic teams. Following are just some of the ways and places to explore leadership opportunities.

Become a Leader of a Club

There are many clubs and organizations that you can join and eventually lead. You may have to work your way up the ladder to become a leader, so get involved early.

Become a Class Officer

If you really want to take on a big leadership role, run for a class officer position at your school. Your school's student government will most likely consist of a president, vice president, treasurer, and secretary. If you're committed to improving student life in school and want to substantially develop your leadership skills, run for office.

Become a Group Leader in Class

Look for leadership opportunities in the classroom. In class, when you are assigned to various projects, volunteer to be the leader of that project team. In addition, many schools offer a leadership or management course. See if you can take a leadership course.

Become a Leader Within Your Part-Time and Summer Jobs

There are some other places to become a leader outside of school. As you work at your part-time and summer jobs, look for leadership opportunities. Talk to your boss about wanting to take on more responsibilities, and see if you can help train new student employees. You can really beef up your part-time experience by taking on a leadership role!

Become a Leader in Your Community

Another place where you can find leadership opportunities is in your local community. Community agencies often need help. Many of these agencies would love to have a student volunteer to head up a certain project. If you are active in any clubs in your community, such as Girl Scouts or Boy Scouts, consider becoming a Scout Leader!

Become a Leader of a Team

If you are on an athletic team, look for opportunities to lead your teammates. Being a team captain is great, but that's not the only way to experience leadership on your team. Talk to your coach about projects such as community service or fundraising efforts, or about leading younger players in off-season workouts. A coach always likes to have players who initiate more involvement with the team!

"Leadership skills are utilized all day by those with good communication skills, good problem-solving skills, great attitudes, a great work ethic, and those who have developed trust and respect among their subordinates. Most companies wish to promote from within, so existing employees realize they'll have a shot at any promotional opportunity if they've proven themselves."

—Top sales rep Mike Logan (retired), Pfizer

Tips on Becoming an Effective Leader

Okay, you learned *why* it's important to be a leader, *how* to become a leader, and *where* to identify leadership opportunities. That's all fine and good, but once you *are* a leader, how do you become a good one? Pursuing the essentials presented in this book, and therefore being the best you, will go a long way in helping you become a good leader. Following are five tips for becoming an effective leader, many which incorporate the essentials.

1. Know Yourself

To be an effective leader, you first have to take an honest look at yourself and determine the strengths and limitations related to your role as a leader. Revisit Chapter 1 and think about the types of interpersonal skills you have and how they will affect your leadership ability. Are you conscientious enough or too much? Do you tend to be tactful in resolving conflicts (as conflicts will most likely occur within your group)? Also, revisit Chapter 2 and identify any biases that may affect you as a leader. Always maintain a high level of integrity and strong character (Chapter 6) while being a leader. Think about how you typically handle adversity and what you'll need to do to lead your group through tough times (Chapter 4). Remember, inside every great leader is a great person. Developing your interpersonal skills, appreciation of diversity, and character will benefit you greatly as a leader!

Student Quote

"Leadership is one of the first qualities employers look for in a potential employee. This is because the employer expects someone with leadership qualities to 'step up to the plate' and accomplish whatever goals needs to be accomplished."

—Kim Brown, recent graduate

2. Remember Your Attentional Profile

Your Attentional Profile (Chapter 7) will have a big effect on your performance as a leader. Good awareness is necessary in reading your group members and being perceptive when a member or members are unhappy with how things are going. You'll need to be aware of the emotions and feelings of your group and have a good sense when things are going well and when they're not. As a leader, you'll also need to be conceptual at times, leading the group in developing a vision and figuring out the best programs to offer. When conflicts occur within the group, you'll need to analyze the problem and offer well-thought-out solutions. Finally, successful leaders are able to focus in on the details that need to take place. You'll have to be responsible in coordinating all the different initiatives, programs, and projects in which your group is involved. You'll need to concentrate on balancing the budget and developing tight meeting agendas. Therefore, you should keep your Attentional Profile in mind and make adjustments to be Aware, Conceptual, and Focused at the appropriate times during your leadership experience!

3. Be a "Democratic" Leader

There are three broad leadership styles: *autocratic*, *laissez-faire*, and *democratic*. Autocratic leaders are similar to dictators, in that they tend to call all the shots and expect the group members to follow. "My way or the highway" is the motto that autocratic leaders live by. The downside to this style of leadership is that the members tend not to be very invested or empowered in reaching goals they had nothing to do in setting. Autocratic leaders not only set the goals themselves, but they tell the group members what they should do and how they should do it. Laissez-faire leaders, on the other hand, are just the opposite. They are "laid back" and pretty much hands-off, allowing group members to do what they want. The problem with this approach is that many groups run all over their laissez-faire leaders with group members going in different directions. Little gets accomplished when a leader isn't very active. A democratic leader is one who brings the entire group into the process of developing a mission and goals, yet actively facilitates discussions and mediates during arguments. A democratic leader also empowers his or her members and respects their individual styles in getting tasks done, yet

> ### Student Quote
>
> "I define leadership as service to others. This does not mean if you are not the president of a club or organization that you are not a leader. You can definitely serve others as just a general member of an organization. When it is time to adjust the course of a club or organization and everyone is okay with the way it is, speak up, keep things changing and growing. If we ever feel that we can't grow with the organization we are with, then we need to find one that will foster our growth as well."
>
> —*Ellery Loomis,*
> *recent graduate*

is happy to advise when asked and steps in when he or she deems necessary. Striking a good balance between being too hands on and not active enough is important in becoming an effective leader!

4. Know Your Group Members

In addition to knowing yourself and remembering your Attentional Profile, you need to get to know your group members as well! What are the strengths that each member brings to the table? What are their weaknesses? Who are the extroverts who talk all the time during meetings, and how can you, the leader, get the introverts to offer more of their thoughts? Which members would be good representatives in public, and which ones will be better at focusing in on the details? Remember, good teams are made up of diverse individuals who offer different skill sets and styles. As a leader, you want to enable your members to utilize their strengths and offer their unique perspectives!

5. Maintain a Healthy Balance

As a leader, it's important to maintain a healthy balance across the following three dynamics.

Dreaming vs. Realistic

It's important to allow your group to dream big and brainstorm creative ideas, but if you want your group to accomplish things, it's also important to be realistic when deciding what and how much can get done. Ask yourself whether you're a dreamer or a doer and how that affects your ability to help your group strike a healthy balance.

Organized vs. Flexible

A second dynamic you should try to balance centers on organization. Yes, as a leader, it's important to come prepared with detailed agendas and organized thoughts, but you also need to be flexible enough to allow for positive changes along the way. Sometimes things come up that alter your original plan, yet are important for your group to adapt to. And remember that you're leading a group of individuals, some of whom may offer different ways of doing things. It's important to be flexible in entertaining these varying views. Many times the surprises in life are the things that make the biggest difference!

Outgoing vs. Listening

You often hear people praise their leaders for being gregarious, outgoing, and a people person. However, it's important that you don't go overboard as a leader. Great leaders are also great listeners. They know when somebody wants to say something important and are able to focus in on what they have to say. If you tend to be a talker, you should consciously make adjustments and learn to listen more during meetings and other group functions. If you tend to be more introverted, you need to challenge yourself to speak up at times and "work the crowd" when your group meets in social settings.

Confronting Issues as a Leader

As we learned in Chapter 4, a true measure of character is how one deals with adversity. Similarly, the success of leaders is often measured by how they handled challenging issues and difficult situations within their groups. In Chapter 3, you learned how to resolve conflicts with another person in a direct, yet tactful way. As a leader, the same concepts apply, yet many times you won't be in conflict with another person; you'll be helping to resolve a conflict occurring among different group members. During these situations, you must try to be fair, impartial, and tactful with all parties involved. And as in any conflict, you as a leader must determine when, where, and how to confront the issue with each of the individuals. Following is a case of a leader, Mike, and how he handled a conflict occurring between two of his group members.

Case Study: A Leader's Role in Resolving Conflicts

What you're about to read are scenes that illustrate various approaches and techniques related to confrontation and conflict resolution. Some of the approaches demonstrate effective confrontation, while others show what not to do when resolving conflicts. Particular emphasis is placed on the leader's role in resolving the conflict both during and after the time of the confrontation.

The setting takes place at a high school. Mike is the president of the junior class and the facilitator of the weekly class officers meetings. Mary is the vice president. Joe is the treasurer in charge of finance and budgets. Mike, Joe, and Mary are in a weekly staff meeting, comprised of seven junior class officers. Joe has become increasingly agitated due to Mary consistently being a day or two late in submitting her monthly budget report. The reports are due by the last day of each month. During one part of the officers meeting, the president (Mike) asks Joe how the budget looks. Joe's response set off some fireworks as you're about to see...

SCENE 1: TAKING SIDES

Joe: Well, if certain people would get their budget reports in on time, I'd be able to crunch the numbers and provide a summary. The last day of each month doesn't mean the second or third of the following month. (Joe looks right at Mary. Mary is very embarrassed, and the rest of the staff members feel awkward.) I need every single budget report submitted on time to do my job—is that clear? I'm just so sick of it!

Mike: Joe's right—we really need everyone to get the reports in on time. Mary, is there anything we can do to help you get your reports in on time?

(Mary gets up and leaves the room; she's embarrassed and upset.)

This first scene showed Mike, the leader, taking sides and further putting Mary on the spot, resulting in Mary becoming humiliated and feeling singled out to the point of having to leave the meeting. We give Mike another shot at handling this confrontation a little more effectively, as you'll see in this next scene.

SCENE 2: DEFERRING THE HEATED ISSUE

Joe: Well, if certain people would get their budget reports in on time, I'd be able to crunch the numbers and provide a summary. The last day of each month doesn't mean the second or third of the following month. (Joe looks right at Mary. Mary is very embarrassed, and the rest of the staff members feel awkward.) I need every single budget report submitted on time to do my job—is that clear? I'm just so sick of it!

Mike: Joe, I need you to settle down. We'll talk about this after the meeting when we can have a more positive discussion about it. We have a lot of other issues that need to be addressed today, and let's start by talking about the upcoming Prom. Ally, would you please provide us with a status report on the Prom? (Mike lets Joe and Mary cool down a bit by turning the meeting over to Ally.)

As you just observed, Mike felt that it was best to postpone this heated topic to a later time and different place and continue with the meeting at hand. What you're now going to read about is what takes place after the meeting. Mike felt it was important to first see how Mary was doing and heads to her locker to speak to her.

SCENE 3: CHECKING IN ON MARY

Mike: Hey Mary, do you have a minute?

Mary: (Upset) Yeah.

Mike: I wanted to see how you're doing.

Mary: (Crying) I'm sorry about not getting the reports in, but I really didn't think it was a big deal. I didn't think Joe did anything with the reports right away.

Mike: Well, don't beat yourself up too much over this. There are multiple issues taking place here as I see it. First, if you know that you consistently have trouble getting the reports in, you may want to talk to Joe and see if he does do something with the reports right away. But frankly, I'm more concerned about the way that Joe confronted the issue. That must not have been pleasant for you this morning during the meeting.

Mary: (still upset) No, it wasn't. I wish Joe would come to me directly when he has an issue with me.

Mike: Well, I'd really like to see you and Joe work on your relationship, specifically how you can communicate more openly about issues. I'm going to talk to Joe about this as well and ask that he initiate a meeting with you to determine how you may work together more effectively. How do you feel about that?

Mary: I think that's a good idea.

Mike: Great. Why don't we check in later to see how your meeting went?

Mary: That sounds great.

After talking to Mary, Mike went to find Joe to get his take on the confrontation and to express to Joe his perspective of what happened and what should take place next.

SCENE 4: CONFRONTING JOE

Mike: Joe, I'd like to talk to you about the meeting this morning. Do you have a minute?

Joe: Yeah, sure.

Mike: I could tell that you were frustrated with the budget reports, and it was obvious that you were directing your frustration to Mary.

Joe: I'm just so sick of having to round up these reports. The deadline is very clear, and everybody else follows it, but Mary always is late.

Mike: Have you talked with Mary about this prior to the meeting?

Joe: No—I don't feel like I should have to babysit her and remind her of this.

Mike: Joe, as the person in charge of budgets, I don't blame you for being frustrated. And I don't blame you for wanting to address your concern. I'd just like you to consider when and where you address your concern, as well as how you confront other staff members. Do you think this was the best way to address the concern?

Joe: I guess not. It just got to me so much, I had to get it out.

Mike: I agree. I don't think this was the best approach. Confronting Mary in front of the other class officers put Mary on the defensive and embarrassed her. Also, the rest of the officers felt awkward, and it was hard for me to lead positive, open discussions after that point. I am a believer of giving individuals the benefit of the doubt by approaching them individually, behind closed doors, and tactfully addressing the issue at hand.

Joe: Yeah, you're right. I need to work on that.

Mike: Well, in moving forward, I'd like to ask you to initiate a meeting with Mary to discuss ways that the two of you can communicate more effectively. I hope that you'll listen to Mary and keep an open mind during this meeting. And frankly, I feel you owe Mary an apology.

Joe: I guess you're right. I'll be sure to schedule a meeting with Mary soon.

In summary, there are a number of points to emphasize:

- Overall, it is critical to determine when, where, and how to confront others.
- Joe hid behind the group to confront Mary. It's usually best to confront a coworker individually.
- This was not the best time nor place to confront (when and where).
- Plus, Joe was not tactful in expressing his concern (how).

Regarding the Leader:

- When a heated confrontation occurs in a group setting or at a staff meeting, the leader shouldn't take sides during the meeting, but encourage the

Student Quote

"Being aware of the things happening around you and working to fix them or standing up for what you believe in is leadership."

—*Brian Jacobs,*
political science major

group to settle down and express the need to discuss the concern later, at a more appropriate time and place.

- The leader should follow up with both parties involved, encouraging them to meet with one another and work out a more healthy working relationship.

- The leader needs to confront individuals who do not tactfully or appropriately confront other members, asking them to take the initiative in working things out with one another.

Leadership Advice from a College Student Government President

MY LEADERSHIP EXPERIENCE

By Mark Gustafson

SGA Executive President

Elon University

"It is time for a new generation of leadership to cope with problems and new opportunities, for there is a new world to be won."

—Former President John F. Kennedy

We will all be leaders at least at one point of our life—captain of a team, lead role in a play, or taking a leadership position in an organization. I am fortunate enough to experience the latter being elected executive president of the Student Government Association at Elon University. So much can be said for what it means to be a leader, but from my experience of being a leader, it is that it helps you grow as a person. It is an amazing feeling to see your organization get better under your leadership; it is a sense of accomplishment. You also get a sense of growth both intellectually and emotionally while learning your limits and how to interact with others.

Leadership is not management. Management and leadership are two different, interrelated, simultaneously occurring processes that are necessary to achieve organizational goals. Management entails the effective and efficient application of resources in order to achieve these goals. This means doing the right things and doing things right. Leadership isn't some sophisticated technique for getting people to do what you want them to do. Leadership is getting people to want to do what you want them to because they share your purpose, vision, and values; it's a matter of influencing behavior.

A part of being a leader is to serve a higher purpose, something other than you. This doesn't necessarily mean that you have to have a formal leadership position, but by serving a higher purpose you are encouraging collaboration, trust, foresight, and listening amongst your peers. You need to act as if you are personally accountable to all of those who are affected by your leadership. This is the new philosophy of servant leadership. Servant leaders serve from the middle and begin by first listening to their peers. As president of the student body, you are a servant for the people and more importantly, a role model. Therefore, you need to establish your honor and reputation through your character and morals.

An important part of being a leader is creating a vision. You need to understand and accept that change is a key element for creating a vision. At the beginning of my term, I proposed a major change to our organization council to make it more representational of all organizations. Prior to this, we only had select organizations on the council representing their personal interests. This proposal was originally met with a lot of animosity. As a leader, you need to listen to other's opinions but show them why change is important—make them see the bigger picture. Also, make sure that you reach out to introverted students who might not feel comfortable giving their opinion unless asked.

Set ideal goals that do not specifically define the final outcome, but are related to an ideal process. A goal is something that can't be evaluated and will span over time. Objectives are measurable steps towards a goal and can be accomplished in a set period of time by selected individuals. Make sure that your goals are SMART—specific, measurable, assignable, realistic, and time-related.

Setting and achieving goals help make your time as a leader more effective and fulfilling. After you have set your goals and objectives for your organization, you need to find an effective way to communicate your vision. Leadership starts with communication. Make sure you do not keep anyone in the dark about what you as an organization are doing.

A leader must also be organized and be able to manage their time wisely. In my case, I am currently involved in SGA, leadership development, a fraternity, and club baseball, not to mention day-to-day school work and classes. Not once has managing my time become an issue. I have to stay organized and manage my time around my priorities—school, work, SGA, clubs, and then hanging out with friends. One of the landmark setbacks of my term was creating a collaborative environment among the SGA Executive Council. Coming from all different backgrounds and personality traits, we had to work through our differences. Compromise is something that can be constructive or destructive. Make sure that you are constructive with your opinions and put emotions aside to see the bigger purpose. Being able to manage and analyze conflict is a fundamental skill for leaders. Make sure to remember that not all conflict is destructive. Learn to see conflict as a way to better understand each other. Don't avoid the problem; try to identify what exactly the problem is. Find areas of agreement, and clarify what is being said and what is meant. Narrow the disagreement down to the smallest problems and work from there. Don't avoid adversity. It is your response to adversity that characterizes you as a

(continued)

(continued)

leader. Although being a leader is very important and time consuming, make sure that you take a break. Always try and look at the larger scheme of things outside of the bubble. Leadership is becoming more and more relationship-oriented. Take the time to get to know those you are going to be working with outside of your working environment. Go to the movies together or get some dinner. Take the time to look within yourself and find out more about who you truly are. Emotions and intellect are complementary. In business, you will need intellect to become a CEO, but it is your emotional intelligence that will make you more effective. Learn to listen to others and gain empathy. When debating issues, I make sure to first understand what the other person is saying before trying to find a solution. Especially when talking to constituents, you really need to learn how to listen. Also realize that sometimes a leader can't solve all the problems, but they can help build a bridge to help them overcome problems and give followers hope.

While in high school, take the opportunity to get involved. It will not only give you experience that will help you in the future, but you will make long-lasting friends on the way. In high school I was involved with student and class council, spirit club, national honor society, and indoor track, and also played baseball. Being so active gave me an opportunity to meet people I probably would not have met, including my best friend. Working within a society, we all have something to give—find your passion and run with it. Give back to your community through volunteering; it is a wonderful humbling experience. Find a role model and learn from watching their leadership styles. It is like the stars in the sky. As you watch the sky, it is when you make patterns that you can find constellations. Much like stars, every time you learn something, make a connection into a pattern, and you'll have a true understanding.

THE WHOLE IN ONE

- Becoming a leader can make you more marketable to college and company recruiters, as well as help you develop a plethora of skills and qualities including initiative, self-confidence, and teamwork.

- The best way to become a leader is to find a group you're excited to join, become active within that group, and then pursue leadership opportunities.

- There are many different groups to lead, including clubs, student government, class project teams, community groups, and athletic teams.

- To be an effective leader, it's helpful to know yourself, remember your Attentional Profile, be a democratic leader, know your group members, and maintain a healthy balance.

- When dealing with conflicts between group members, you must determine when, where, and how to confront each of the members involved.
- Take advice from a leader like Mark Gustafson, former President of the Student Government at Elon University.

BECOME THE BEST YOU...BECOME A LEADER!

Chapter 8 Review

Read each question and circle the *best* answer.

1. **The following are characteristics of leaders except**

    a. initiative.

    b. organizational skills.

    c. self-confidence.

    d. bossiness.

2. **In the author's case study of Stephanie, what experience started her on the way to being a leader?**

    a. Joining a club she was passionate about

    b. Joining the most respected club in the school

    c. Joining the swim team

    d. Joining a club that her friends belonged to

3. **When a heated confrontation occurs in a peer meeting, the leader should**

    a. calm both parties down and encourage them to talk it over.

    b. calm both parties down and encourage them to talk it over at another time.

    c. encourage the two parties to discuss the matter until there is a positive result.

    d. solve the matter him- or herself.

4. **Leaders should know that it is critical to determine _____ to confront others. All of these are correct except**

    a. when.

    b. how.

    c. why.

    d. where.

5. **A synonym for *gregarious* is**

    a. serious.

    b. outgoing.

    c. introvert.

    d. silly.

6. **A true measure of character is how one deals with**

   a. adversity.

   b. people.

   c. students.

   d. anger.

7. **What is the best definition of an *autocratic* leader?**

   a. One who allows his/her group to make most of the decisions

   b. One who makes the agenda and allows the group to partake in the decision making

   c. One who sets up the meeting and then allows others to lead it

   d. One who not only sets the goals but tells people how they should attain them

8. **One who is a "laid-back" leader is called**

   a. a laissez-faire leader.

   b. a democratic leader.

   c. a autocratic leader.

   d. all of the above.

9. **Good _____ is/are crucial in leading your group members.**

   a. humor

   b. listening skills

   c. awareness

   d. focus

10. **To become a leader of a group, a person should**

   a. "take the reins" right away.

   b. speak about a topic in front of a group.

   c. study everything there is to know about a topic.

   d. earn the group's respect by being a productive member.

9

Career and Character Education
Essential #9

Connect to the World Around You

"When evaluating an applicant, the Peace Corps considers the 'whole person' including your life experiences, community involvement, volunteer work, motivations, and even your hobbies. In most cases, applicants with a bachelor's degree in any discipline, strong motivation, and a commitment to Peace Corps service will be competitive to become Peace Corps Volunteers. However, relevant internships will help to set the applicant apart from the crowd."

—Peace Corps

Get Out There and Become "Worldly"

To become the best you, it is important to be in touch with and engaged in the world around you! Successful people don't hibernate in a small cubicle, oblivious to the world around them. They get out and get involved in many areas of interest. In short, the best you is a worldly you! A *worldly person* is someone who is connected to the communities and world around him; who cares about the issues and challenges facing our world; who gets involved in causes that he values; who understands both the importance of work and the importance of contributing to society. You've probably heard adults talk about how students aren't in the "real world." Well, in many ways, this statement is simply not true. As a student, you *are* experiencing success, failure, joy, sorrow, and every other emotion found in the real world. Where the world of many students is not "real" is in the lack of connection with work, politics, and service. This is the time in your life to change that and begin getting connected!

Connecting with the World of Work

Let's begin with the world of work. To become the best you, it's important to start gaining a better understanding of how the working world operates. If you plan on going to college, recruiters like to see that you've gained some work experience. Participating in part-time work, internships, or apprenticeships looks good on a college application and can help you clarify what you may want to major in. Plus, during college admission interviews, you'll be able to talk more intelligently about the world of work because you are involved in it. If you don't plan on going to college, then you'll likely be entering the workforce. Company recruiters want to hire graduates who have experience working. Many will hire you based on your performance in a previous apprenticeship. Just as important, though, through participating in the world of work, you will become enlightened about a very important aspect of our society—work!

The following are the best ways to connect with the world of work on your way to becoming more connected with your world.

> ## Student Quote
>
> "Being an intern shows you the daily routine of someone in that profession. My senior year of high school, I had an internship with a local middle school math teacher. I would spend two or three days a week with him, watching him teach and helping him with his lesson plans. Because of this experience I discovered that I really didn't want to be a math teacher and that the daily tasks of a teacher, from a teacher's point of view as opposed to a student's point of view, were much different than I expected."
>
> —*Kim Brown, recent graduate*

Internships/Apprenticeships

The best way for you to get connected to the world of work is through internships or apprenticeships. An *internship* or *apprenticeship* is a hands-on work experience that provides training in a career area you're considering. The term *apprenticeship* tends to be used more within the trades, such as carpentry and auto mechanics, whereas the term *internship* is used more in business, health care, and education. Because referring to both experiences (internship/apprenticeship) is somewhat cumbersome, from here on we'll primarily use the term internship, but please remember we're referring to both! An internship provides an opportunity for you to "test the waters" and experience a career firsthand. This benefits you in three main ways. First, by working for months within one career field, you get a really good sense of whether this career is one that you'd like to pursue later on. It helps clarify your career plans! Second, the level of work experience you gain makes you that much more marketable to college or company recruiters. This is the most relevant career experience you can gain as a student! Third, an internship helps you become more knowledgeable about the workforce, thus connecting you to the world around you.

"It is important for our company to hire graduates who have had internships or co-op experiences because that allows those individuals to gain knowledge of the kind of work we are involved in as well as real-world experiences. My experience over the last 12 years tells me that most college graduates do not have enough real-world experience. In most cases college graduates have gone from elementary, middle, and high school and their home life to college life. Then from college life they are dumped into the marketplace with little real-world experience. Internships and co-ops are a great way to gain those experiences."

—Jefferson Pilot

Participating in an internship or apprenticeship is the best way to get connected to the working world and to gain experience. By working for a period of months at a time, you get to know a number of company employees and experience a job and career field firsthand. However, there are other less-extensive ways to get connected to the world of work. Here are three other ways that can get you connected.

Information Interviews

Information interviews are meetings or conversations you have with people in careers of interest. You interview (ask questions of) the professionals to gain more information about their careers. Doing this is a great way to learn more about the world of work!

Work Shadowing

You know the saying, "A picture is worth a thousand words." Well, that is at the essence of work shadowing. Through observation and discussions with professionals, you will get a good feel whether their line of work is for you. You will also learn a lot about the working world in general, just by hanging around and watching various companies in action.

Part-Time Jobs

Sometimes part-time jobs can feel very much like an internship. However, the main difference lies in the quality or substance of what you are doing. In theory, internships and apprenticeships are intended to be training experiences where you're sampling real work you would do later in your career. Most students, on the other hand, do part-time jobs to make a little money for themselves—not necessarily to prepare for their careers. However, if you choose your part-time and summer jobs wisely, they can be a good way to get connected to the world of work and sample careers. What you are doing may not be too exciting, but there is nothing wrong with doing a little grunt work or being a gofer occasionally. Also, if you are doing that grunt work for a company in a career field of interest, there is great potential to turn that gofer job into a career-enhancing opportunity. In between the grunting and gofering, sit down and chat with the employees. Ask to meet with various professionals and interview them. Also, see if there is a more-substantial project that needs to be done and volunteer to assist with that project. Take initiative and make the most of your part-time jobs.

Creative Approaches to Connect to the World of Work

Be creative in connecting with the world of work. There are so many different ways to connect as students. I want to share a story of a very creative high school student.

During a career counseling session with her school counselor, Mary, a junior, expressed a desire to learn more about a few career fields in which she was interested: public relations, advertising, and marketing. Mary wanted to know how she could learn more about these fields and gain some contacts as well. After discussing various options, her school counselor mentioned to Mary that she might be able to research these three fields of interest as part of one of her research papers or projects in school. Mary loved the idea. She thought of a project in her social studies class where she could pick what she wanted to research. Mary met with her social studies teacher, and the two of them agreed on what she would do. Her goal was to conduct information interviews with five professionals in each of the three career fields of interest, for a total of 15 information interviews. The school counselor helped Mary identify these 15 contacts.

At the end of the project, Mary came back to meet with her school counselor; she was elated. She said that it was one of the greatest experiences of her high school career. She learned so much about each of the fields and was therefore able to make a sound choice on what she wanted to pursue in college: public relations. In addition to that, she established 15 great contacts in the field. She said she received three summer internship offers, one of which she accepted. This was a great way for Mary to get connected to the world of work. You can do the same.

Engaging in Community Service and Politics

"The soldiers' desire to serve goes beyond their jobs. After duty hours, many coach Little League teams in various sports, participate in running scouting programs, and teach Sunday school. Many soldiers and their spouses volunteer to assist in the Wounded Warrior Program. To them, service is synonymous with responsibility."

—Colonel Art Bair (Retired), U.S. Army

Connecting to the world of work is a great start to becoming more worldly. However, the world of *work* isn't the only "world" with which you should be in contact. The worlds of community service (volunteer) and public service (politics) are just as important! Without active participation in community and public service, our society wouldn't be half as strong as it is today. The only way to really understand our world is to begin learning about the issues and challenges facing our society, and there's no better "classroom" than getting involved in community and public service!

Connect to Your Local Community Through Community Service

"What a person does with their spare time is as important as what they do on the job. Always make time to help the less fortunate by getting involved in the United Way, Big Brothers/Sisters, etc. This shows caring and sacrifice. And remember—helping others helps *you*; you learn, you grow, you lead, and you take ownership of a special opportunity."

—Top sales rep Mike Logan (retired), Pfizer

Seek out volunteer and community service opportunities that interest you. Most schools provide such opportunities. Often times the athletic team or extracurricular group you've joined will coordinate community service projects. They may be helping younger kids in the community, or spending time with the elderly, or working with people with disabilities. Boy Scouts and Girl Scouts are good examples of clubs outside of school which are involved in community service. Remember, whichever group you join, you will be working together with your peers on a common cause. There's really no greater experience than participating in community service! Think about it—you are helping people in need, but you, in turn, are developing skills that employers and colleges are looking for and skills that will help you be the best you. All the while, you're becoming more in touch with the world around you.

Student Quote

"Public service is giving of yourself because it is the right thing to do and because we can touch others just by lending a helping hand. When I graduated from high school, we were required to participate in hours of community service; I do not recall how many, but I do recall they began keeping track in seventh grade. This was an opportunity for us to give back to the community that supports the school system every day. I believe that every high school student should engage in public service. In my mind, a person should not be judged by the actions the world sees, but the actions the world does not see."

—*Ellery Loomis, recent graduate*

ON A PERSONAL NOTE...

As a freshman in college, I signed up for the Big Brother program. I was assigned to a young boy in the local community who had no real father figure. I didn't have a car on campus. However, every Sunday that year, while my buddies were watching football, I'd beg someone to drive me over to see my little brother. I spent every Sunday afternoon playing and talking with him. We kept in touch over the years, and he is now a successful member of the military. I look back on that experience, and without a doubt, it is the experience of which I am most proud.

This volunteer experience also broadened my perspective on the world. Growing up, I lived in a very nice neighborhood, was raised by two highly educated parents, and had friends who were really good kids. My little brother wasn't as fortunate. He lived in a run-down neighborhood; was raised by a single mother who was in and out of relationships; and hung out with kids who were smoking, drinking, and always getting into trouble. It opened my eyes to a world that was very different from mine, making me appreciate more what I had while feeling sorry for those who weren't so lucky. Having this experience gave me a dose of reality that I needed to become less naïve and a bit more in touch with the world around me!

Engage in the Political Issues and Challenges Facing Our World Today

History, political science, and social studies aren't always students' favorite classes. Many students especially wonder why they need to take history and learn about things that happened a hundred years ago. Well, what you have to start understanding is that things don't happen in one moment of time. There's a cause and effect to everything. What happened a hundred years ago affects how we view the world today. To completely understand the issues and challenges today, we must understand what happened "yesterday."

So, the first thing you should do is pay closer attention in history and political science–type classes. Don't just memorize the dates and issues and spit them back out come test time. Try to understand the importance of what happened in the past and how that affected the issues and challenges today. Likewise, don't just learn that there's a Democratic party, a Republican party, a Senate, and a Congress. Learn what the people from both the Democratic and Republican parties believe in, and start identifying what you believe in as well! Stay current on issues facing the Senate and Congress (on the state level as well as on the national level).

Student Quote

"I was especially involved in my community during high school. Besides helping others, it makes you feel better about yourself and expands your interests. I guarantee that as soon as you get involved in community service in one place you will make connections to other ways to serve your community."

—*Michelle Kelly, education major*

"Often our community is a microcosm of our world of work. Community service provides another lens into how this person operates/functions in a complex environment. Certainly, such service demonstrates an interest to be involved and committed to a cause. This gives us more confidence that the person will take ownership and responsibility. It also demonstrates a capacity for passion, which as oddly as it sounds, many people often do not have—they are simply satisfied with the 'status quo' and not interested in moving the ball forward."

—Smart and Associates, LLP

Next, explore ways to get involved in politics outside the classroom. See if there is a "Young Republicans" or "Young Democrats" club through your school or somewhere else in the community. See if you can get involved in constructive debates in school. Joining the Debate Team is a great way to deeply learn about the issues and to start forming your strong beliefs. Also, when you're at home, ask your parents what they believe in and why they believe that way. Ask what's going on in the news locally, nationally, and throughout the world. Remember, you are living in a world that offers news 24/7 (i.e., CNN, Headline News, etc.). Join a political blogging community and engage in the conversation. When election time is near, talk to your parents about whom they're supporting and why they're supporting them. If your friends or peers in school bring up politics, jump right in on the conversations. Just remember, as you become more knowledgeable about the issues and begin to engage more in politics, it's important to utilize the other essentials you learned previously in the book: interpersonal skills, teamwork, appreciation of diversity, etc. Not everybody believes what you believe, so it's important to listen hard, respect differences, and express your opinions and beliefs tactfully.

Travel

Another way to get connected with your world is to get out there and see it when you have the chance. When your family travels across the country or to different countries, realize that this is a great opportunity for you to learn more firsthand about the various societies around you and to gain a broader perspective of the

Student Quote

"Volunteering and being charitable aren't just great activities to have on your resume; they change who you are, as a person, and make you truly appreciate what you have. I can truly say that my life was changed when I spent two weeks building houses for people who couldn't afford housing in Georgia one summer."

—Kim Brown,
recent graduate

Student Quote

"As a student, find an internship opportunity in something you are interested in and use the resources available to you. If your school/college has an internship coordinator, ask them for assistance or talk to your advisor. Use books and the Internet to look for internships. I learned things from my internships that I never learned from a textbook or in the classroom. It is up to you to find an internship–don't expect one to fall in your lap."

—Michelle Ford,
communication arts major

world. Soak in the environment, ask a million questions, and learn to appreciate the exciting differences that exist from city to city, state to state, and nation to nation. Learn about the different ethnic, racial, and religious cultures as you travel. If there is an opportunity to travel or become an exchange student, take a serious look into it! A big part of becoming more worldly is traveling to different places and experiencing the various cultures.

Your Getting Connected Plan

The World of Work

The careers that I am interested in are the following:

_____

_____

I am going to become better connected to the world of work and learn more about careers of interest through doing the following.

Internships/Apprenticeships:

_____

_____

_____

Work Shadowing:

_____

_____

_____

Information Interviewing:

_____

_____

_____

(continued)

(continued)

Part-time Jobs:

_____

_____

_____

Community Service

In the past, I have volunteered my time in the community in the following ways:

_____

_____

_____

In the future, I would like to become involved in community service in the following ways:

_____

_____

_____

Political Issues and Public Service

The political issues that I'm currently aware of are the following:

_____

_____

_____

I know the following political leaders.

Local Leaders (i.e., my community's mayor):

_____

_____

_____

State Leaders (i.e., my state's governor and senators):

_____

_____

_____

National Leaders (i.e., my nation's president, vice president, secretary of defense):

_____

_____

_____

International Leaders (i.e., other nations' presidents and key political leaders):

_____

_____

I plan on learning more about the issues and politics by doing the following:

_____

_____

_____

Travel

In the past, I have traveled to the following places:

_____

_____

_____

In the future, I hope to travel to the following places:

_____

_____

_____

THE WHOLE IN ONE

- To be the best you, you should be connected to the world and communities around you. Work, community service, politics, and travel help you become connected.
- There are multiple ways to become connected to the world of work:
  - Conduct information interviews with professionals in careers that interest you.
  - Observe professionals in action through work shadowing and during part-time jobs.
  - Experience career options directly through internships, apprenticeships, and certain part-time jobs.
- Get connected to your surrounding community through community service—there's nothing like it!
- Become aware of the issues, politics, and leaders within your local, state, and federal government. Analyze and debate important issues with friends, family members, and peers!
- Get out there and travel! Learn about the many wonderful cultures that make this world an exciting place.

BECOME THE BEST YOU...CONNECT TO THE WORLD AROUND YOU!

Chapter 9 Review

Read each question and circle the *best* answer.

1. **What does "being engaged in the world around you" mean?**

   a. Hibernating in a small cubicle

   b. Experiencing every part of your job equally

   c. Getting involved in many areas of interest

   d. Being a part of the "real world"

2. **For high school graduates, company recruiters want to hire graduates who have experience**

   a. speaking.

   b. working.

   c. driving.

   d. writing.

3. ***Apprenticeship* is to *trades* as *internship* is to**

   a. business.

   b. schools.

   c. outside work.

   d. desk jobs.

4. **"Test the waters" is an example of what kind of figurative language?**

   a. Simile

   b. Analogy

   c. Metaphor

   d. Idiom

5. **Which definition best defines *marketable*?**

   a. Better

   b. Improved

   c. More appealing

   d. Experienced

(continued)

(continued)

6. **Participating in a/an _____ is the best way to get connected to the working world and gain experience.**

   a. internship

   b. club

   c. sport

   d. charity

7. **Meetings with people in careers of interest are called _____**

   a. part-time jobs.

   b. internships.

   c. information interviews.

   d. work shadowing.

8. **Why did the author include Mary's experience in his book?**

   a. To show students that anyone can get an internship

   b. To show students that if you want something done, do it yourself

   c. To show students that part-time jobs are very good experiences

   d. To show students that there are creative ways to learn about jobs

9. **Why did the author include his Big Brother experience in this chapter?**

   a. To show what an internship can do for a person

   b. To show the positive relationship he and his little brother had

   c. To show how his experience made him a more worldly person

   d. To show how great of a person he is

10. **You should travel**

    a. to gain a broader perspective of the world.

    b. to learn firsthand about the various societies around you.

    c. to find yourself.

    d. both a and b.

Career and Character Education
Essential #10

Become an Active Explorer

"We are a fast-paced organization that looks to people to be able to learn quickly. We have found that those graduates who have explored and worked in professional environments prior to graduation have shorter learning curves than those who don't. As the old saying goes, 'Time is money.' The less time it takes for someone to learn, the quicker they become productive. In addition, there are primary professional skills and abilities that are only learned by being a part of an organization. Internships and co-ops in particular help an individual learn what it is like to be in a professional environment."

—PricewaterhouseCoopers

You Can Only Choose from What You Know

Robert Frost wrote, "Two roads diverged in a wood, and I...I took the one less traveled, and that has made all the difference." Unfortunately, when making important life decisions, most teens aren't exposed to "the road less traveled" and are forced to make decisions based only on those options that have become familiar to them. For example, if you're looking to buy a music CD, chances are you'll buy a CD that a friend told you about or that you heard on the radio or online. Out of the thousands of CDs that are out there, it's likely that there's one that would be perfect for you, but because you haven't been exposed to it, you wouldn't buy it. Similarly, most students choose a career based on the small number of options to which they have been exposed. People have been choosing careers in this manner for a long time. Look at what Dr. Charles Moore, author of *The Career Game*, wrote in 1976, and then what Dr. Jack Rayman, Director of Career Services at Penn State University, wrote more than 25 years later in 2002:

MOORE, 1976

"It became clear that most of the students who already had prospective career fields in mind had unnecessarily narrowed their initial career selections rather arbitrarily and haphazardly. The federal government's *Dictionary of Occupational Titles* lists 35,000 separate vocational categories. Nevertheless, I found that most students who selected a career had selected it from among a handful of opportunities they had become familiar with largely through chance circumstances. Some had chosen their major simply because of the rapport they had with a particular professor. Or their parents, relatives, or someone else had decided for them. Most of them knew too little about themselves. Their knowledge of specific career opportunities was limited in most cases to a shallow understanding of their parents', relatives', and friends' occupations and miscellaneous facts they had picked up here and there. Virtually none of these students understood how to approach their career decision strategically."

Source: The Career Game. *Ansonia Station, NY: National Institute of Career Planning.*

RAYMAN, 2002

"Today's students don't realize that there are more than 22,000 different jobs available within the U.S. economy. Most students' knowledge of the world of work is based on superficial mass media exposure to a relatively small number of unrepresentative jobs. A surprising number of students don't even know what their parents do for a living. Unfortunately, as a society, we still do a relatively poor job of providing our sons and daughters with exposure to the thousands of different exciting career possibilities that exist. In my opinion the chief obstacle to the consideration of a broader, more representative range of career options is the lack of exposure. We are little removed from a caste structure with respect to occupational choice. It is still the case that far too many students enter the same occupation as their parents, not because it is an appropriate choice, but because they simply don't know what else is available."

Source: Adapted from "The Changing Role of Career Services," New Direction for Student Services, Number 62, Summer 1993, Jossey-Bass, San Francisco.

Actively Explore Your Options—Your Future Depends on It!

You will be faced with many important decisions in your life that have a big impact on who you become. It's been said that *you make decisions, and then the decisions make you.* In order to become the best you, it's critical to be active in exploring your options when you have an important decision to make. Take a look at the following scenario—buying a car—and notice the five steps used in actively exploring the options.

A Model for Actively Exploring: Buying a Car

Let's think ahead about an exciting decision that you'll be making some day—deciding on the right car to buy. There are hundreds and hundreds of cars out there from which to choose; expensive, economical, sporty, practical, big, small, convertibles, SUVs, etc. How can you possibly check out each one? Well, you can't. Therefore, you start by thinking of important things you want in a car, thus eliminating hundreds of others out there (Step 1). You may say, "I want a sporty car with fewer than 30,000 miles on it. And it can't cost more

> ### Student Quote
>
> "By constantly seeking what career path you are interested in during high school, you can truly make your life easier when you get to college. First and most obvious, you can save a ton of money by knowing your interests. You can tailor your first-year courses to fit into a major that interests you. This will save you the time and expense of changing majors. Secondly, having your areas of interest in hand, your college or institution can be looking at introducing you to members of that professional field. Again, this continues to assist you in ensuring that you have chosen the field that will make you happy. Find something that you can do for the rest of your life, have passion for it, and love what you do!"
>
> —Ellery Loomis, recent graduate

than $25,000." You have narrowed down your choices and begun focusing in on a certain category of cars. Now what?

Well, you first want to start reading up on your options (Step 2). You can pick up brochures from various local car dealerships and browse through them. Lately, more and more people are heading to the Internet to check out cars. Either way, you will start identifying models of cars that fit your criteria, and you'll read whatever blurbs are available in the brochures or Internet sites. You can take it a step further and read up on these models of interest in various automobile consumer reports. You will get the good and the bad of every car in which you are interested. Well, are you done? Is this all you need to do to buy the car of your dreams? Not usually. Most people are not ready to plunk down thousands of dollars on a car solely from reading a brochure!

The next step may be for you to start asking questions about some of these car prospects (Step 3). You could talk to a friend or family member who knows more about cars than you do. Alternatively, you can simply call a car dealership to speak with a salesperson and ask questions about the cars you're interested in. After you get the opinions of other people and get some of your questions answered, you should be ready to buy a car, right? Not really. At this point, most people are still not prepared to buy a car. What's left to do? You'll probably want to go to one or more of the local car dealerships and get a firsthand look at these vehicles (Step 4). Therefore, you head over to a car lot, and you go over to the section of the lot where the type of car you are looking for will be. You look closely over each car, checking out the color, the shape, the interior, and of course, the price. Usually a car salesperson will spot you and start hanging around. You can get more information from the salesperson.

Remember, this is only the first car dealership you have visited. This process may repeat itself multiple times. Anyway, after all of this—surfing the Internet, reading up on cars, talking to friends, asking questions to car salespeople, and getting a firsthand look yourself at many different cars—you're still not ready to make the final decision. There is typically one last step: the test drive (Step 5). Most car buyers are not ready to buy a car until they check it out firsthand and take it for a test drive! Look at all that is done in order to actively explore cars and make an educated decision on buying the right one.

No matter what you're deciding—what college to attend, what club to join, what internship to acquire, or what career to choose—make sure that you go through the five steps identified in the car model in order to actively explore your options and make good decisions!

The Five Steps of an Active Explorer:

1. **Identify** important criteria of your options.

2. **Read** about your options.

3. **Talk** to people about your options.

4. **Look** at your options.

5. **Experience** your options directly.

Actively Exploring Careers

The five-step model for actively exploring is easy to see in the car example and should be applied to all of the important decisions in your life. One of the most important decisions you will be making is choosing a career. As mentioned in Chapter 6, you will be changing jobs and careers many more times than your parents and grandparents did, so it's extra important that you know how to make informed career decisions! Therefore, our remaining points related to being an active explorer will be applied to deciding on a career. Following is a breakdown of the five-step model as it relates to choosing a career.

Step 1: Identify Important Criteria You Want in a Career

The first thing you must do in deciding on a career is to reflect on your past and assess yourself. In the career world, this process is called *self-assessment*. Remember, there are more than 20,000 occupations out there. To begin narrowing down and focusing in on a more manageable number, you must identify what's important to you in a career and eliminate thousands of options that don't fit.

This self-assessment process can be broken down into four main areas: skills, interests, values, and personal qualities. Simply put, skills are things you're good at (speaking, organizing, drawing, etc.), interests are things you enjoy doing (writing, music, sports, etc.), values are what's important to you (family, money, prestige, etc.), and personal qualities are characteristics that best represent who you are (funny, outgoing, caring, etc.).

Student Quote

"Ask your parents' friends or friends' parents who work in fields you might be interested in. Start off by interviewing them, and then ask if you can come along for a day to see what it is like in their workplace. Ask your school counselor about local connections to places of your career interests and work your way from there."

—*Michelle Kelly, education major*

Talk to your school counselor to see what types of self-assessment instruments and exercises your school offers, and take full advantage of them! It's very important that you're honest with yourself in identifying your skills, interests, values, and qualities. Too many students kid themselves into believing that they are something that they are not. Another important point to remember is that you should always have a professional career counselor or school counselor help you interpret the results of any self-assessment instrument. These counselors are trained to properly interpret these instruments.

Step 2: Read About Career Options of Interest

Now that you have identified your skills, interests, personal qualities, and values, you have eliminated hundreds and hundreds of career options and narrowed your search. The next step to choosing a career that is right for you is to read about those careers that interest you. Too often, the title of a career sounds good, but after you read more about it, you may determine that it's not a good fit.

Books About Exploring Careers

The most traditional way to read about careers is to pick up a book. Several books out there describe a wide variety of careers. Two main types of books exist. First, there are the all-inclusive, comprehensive books that will present hundreds of career options. Two of the most highly used books of this kind have historically been *Occupational Outlook Handbook* and *O*NET Dictionary of Occupational Titles*, both available from JIST Publishing based on U.S. Department of Labor data.

If you don't really have a single career field of interest, these comprehensive books are a good start. However, if you have a career in mind, you may want to read the second type of book: the field-specific career exploration books. Many books out there describe occupations within one particular career field. They will be titled something similar to *Careers in Biology* or *Sociology Jobs*.

Most of the career exploration books provide a general overview of the career, education and training required, job availability outlook, salary and earnings, and other useful information. Check with your career education coordinator or school counselor to see what types of career exploration books they have.

> ### Student Quote
>
> "There are often many clubs and activities you can get involved with after school where you can actively explore areas of interest. Get involved with them. Sitting around the house and watching television or playing video games is not very conducive to anything in the long run."
>
> —Brian Jacobs,
> political science major

Web Sites for Researching Careers

As you may have guessed, there are plenty of Web sites that enable you to read up on and explore careers. The nice thing about the Internet is that it can spice up this process of exploring careers because it's not just one-dimensional. These sites often add graphics, pictures, and video clips. Two examples of good sites are www.jobweb.com and www.bls.gov. The U.S. Department of Labor (DOL) and its Bureau of Labor Statistics (BLS) provide future projections regarding careers that will be in demand. Again, check with your school to see what Internet sites they recommend. Also, check out the career center's Web page of your area college or community college. Most career center Web pages include a section related to exploring careers that's open to the public as well. Follow these links to learn about careers in which you are interested. The other thing you can do is simply run a search on a search engine such as www.yahoo.com or www.google.com. Simply type in something similar to "exploring careers" or, if you have a specific career field in mind, such as human services, just type in "careers in human services".

Step 3: Talk to People in Careers of Interest

The third step in actively exploring career options is to talk to professionals in careers of interest. We call this *information interviewing*, because you will be interviewing professionals for information. Information interviews can be conducted either in person or over the phone. Some information interviews are even conducted via e-mail these days. Talk to your school counselors to see if they know of people in the community that you can information interview. Also, ask your parents if they know of anybody in the careers you're most interested in.

There is some strategy associated with conducting information interviews. The worst thing you could do is jump right into asking the person you're interviewing about internships or jobs he or she may have for you. One of the main goals of information interviewing is to build strong relationships with contacts in your career field of interest. The best way to ensure building strong relationships is to follow the **POWER** Model of information interviewing. Establish a solid list of questions using the progression that follows.

The POWER Model

P: Person you are interviewing

O: Organization of your contact

W: Work field of contact

E: Exploration of opportunities with their company or within the field

R: Referrals to other contacts and organizations

You should start your line of questioning around the **P**erson you are interviewing. Ask how your contact got to where he or she is today and what he or she likes and dislikes about the job. Next, ask questions about the **O**rganization for which your contact works. Ask about the structure of the organization and who their competitors are. Then move to questions related to the **W**ork field in general. Ask questions about current trends and challenges in the career field. Now that you have built a stronger rapport by asking about them, it is now appropriate to **E**xplore opportunities for yourself. Ask about internships or entry-level jobs for which you may be suited and ask advice on how to pursue these opportunities. Finally, you should never leave an information interview without asking for **R**eferrals to colleagues and other organizations in the field. Ask if there is anyone else he or she would recommend you talking with.

Step 4: Take a Look at Your Career Options: Work Shadowing

The fourth step in the exploration process is to get a closer look at your career options of interest. We call this *work shadowing*. Work shadowing is when you tag along with or shadow professionals at work. You can shadow them for a few hours, a day, a week, or sometimes longer. While you do not get to experience or perform the work directly, you do get to be at the work site and observe what goes on within that career field and company.

Make sure you are at your best during the work-shadowing experience. Ask questions and meet as many people as you can. At the end, ask about possible internships with their company. If you presented yourself well, they may be willing to set up an internship with you. Finally, be sure to send a thank-you letter for allowing you to work shadow them. Make sure to visit your career education center or school counselor to see whether your school has a work-shadowing program.

> ### *Student Quote*
>
> "Waiting until college to explore areas of interest in career goals can prove not only to be very tedious but also very expensive. High school is the time to discover a new range of experiences in the job field so that when you enter college you can do all that you can to develop yourself in your field. Use your time in high school to try new things so that your college time and effort is not wasted and so you can focus on being an academically minded, conscientious student."
>
> —*Jennifer Watkavitch,*
> *recent graduate*

Step 5: Experience Careers Directly— Internships/Co-ops/Apprenticeships

There's no better way to explore careers than to experience them directly for a period of time. Essentially you are "test driving" a career to see if you like it. Many schools provide internship or apprenticeship opportunities to their students, so go and look into it!

Why Internships Are So Important

"The internship program is a key recruitment strategy for Verizon to hire the best talent. Working with interns is a long-term investment for the company in realizing permanent employees. Interns are recruited in a manner similar to how full-time employees are recruited. Through the internship program, the company is able to observe the students—look at the skills they've developed, see what they've learned, and assess what they might contribute to the company's future and its goals. The greatest return on investment is when an intern becomes a permanent employee."

—Verizon

Internships have always been important to companies. They are a good way to evaluate students and hire those with some relevant experience. However, internships appear to be even more important today than they have been in the past. When I was the Director of the Elon University career center, I went along with the Dean of the Business School to build relationships with companies in the Washington, D.C., and Baltimore, Maryland, area. After visiting approximately 20 company recruiters, we learned just how important internships and co-ops have become. Nearly 90 percent of the recruiters said that because graduates are changing jobs more frequently and leaving their first job sooner than before, recruiters want to do a better job of screening entry-level candidates. Thus, they are trying to position themselves and their internship program in such a way that they will only hire entry-level candidates from their pool of previous interns.

This idea makes sense. If it was your job to recruit top-quality graduates with all of the essential skills (interpersonal, teamwork, communication, etc.), it is likely that you would prefer to select a candidate from the pool of interns with whom you worked and whom you observed for months rather than an interview candidate that you got to know for less than one day. It is impossible to assess the work ethic, reliability, perseverance, and appreciation for diversity that a candidate possesses from a three-hour interview. When you serve as a company intern for three or four months, the company gets to see how well you get along with coworkers, whether you came to work on time, how you handled conflicts with others, and whether you followed through on tasks.

Student Quote

"Become involved in everything that you can. If you like to sing but don't think you are the type of person who is involved in the school musical, try out anyway! You may find it to be one of your more memorable experiences from high school. And if it isn't, you will have gained knowledge about yourself so you will know what interests to pursue as you get older."

—Kristi Geist, management major

"In many cases the hiring manager may assign a new hire to a project based on their previous experience as an intern or co-op. It's one indicator for many of us to really assess a student's interest or passion in a particular area."

—IBM

Look at the following two statistics taken from the *2008 NACE Job Outlook Survey* conducted by the National Association of Colleges and Employers. These statistics strongly reinforce the importance and effectiveness of internship programs.

1. Employers Rate Effectiveness of Recruiting Methods

   Out of 18 methods for recruiting graduates, two of the top four (rated "very effective") were "Organization's Internship Program" and "Organization's Co-op Program." In other words, organizations love to hire graduates who have worked for them in the past as an intern or co-op student.

2. Employers' Hiring Preferences Relative to Experience

   A compelling 76.2% of organizations "prefer to hire candidates with relevant work experience." Only 18.2% said that they "prefer to hire candidates with *any* type of experience." The best type of "relevant work experience" is internships and co-ops.

Source: 2008 NACE Job Outlook Survey, *National Association of Colleges and Employers*

Make the Most of the Internship

After you are all set and you begin your internship or apprenticeship, it is important that you make the most out of this invaluable experience. Remember, many companies hire previous interns for full-time jobs. This is your time to shine, and using the life essentials we've talked about in this book will certainly help you do just that! Show up on time, be nice to all your new coworkers, get your work done ahead of time, and volunteer to do more than what is expected of you. Also, make sure to reflect on your internship experience whether you

Student Quote

"Colleges are making it more and more difficult for students to graduate in four years, and with tuition on the increase, that can prove to be very costly. Oftentimes when students get to college and are deep into a curriculum of study, they then realize that their chosen career path is not suited for them. High school is the time to gain that on-the-job experience through internships to affirm career goals that may be uncertain."

—Jennifer Watkavitch, recent graduate

are required to or not. Maintain a weekly log, expressing what you like, dislike, and value, as well as the new things that you are learning. In addition, become exposed to the different divisions or departments that exist in the company. Initiate meetings with the directors overseeing the various divisions to learn more about the company. Doing this not only enhances your learning, but it enables you to build more networking contacts for the future. You never know who may take a liking to you. Get out there and meet as many people as you can.

Reflect on the Experience and Re-evaluate Your Career Goals

After the internship is over, make sure to reflect on the experience while it is still fresh. Were you able to use the skills and qualities you enjoy using? Was the work that you performed important or valuable? How did you like the work atmosphere? Is this an environment in which you could see yourself working? Schedule an appointment with your school counselor. Talk to your counselor about your experience and how it may have affected your original career goals.

"Graduates with internship or co-op experience are able to shorten the learning curve, effectively increasing their speed to productivity. This provides a tremendous benefit to both Microsoft and the student because of a reduced need for initial job training."

—Microsoft

Become a Life-Long Learner!

Actively exploring your options is not a one-time thing. As the world of work continues to change, you must be able to adapt with it. So, as you explore new ventures, remember that, in many cases, you'll need to learn new skills and broaden your knowledge base. In short, to be the best you, you must embrace the concept of "life-long learning"! The days when you pick up a trade or diploma and work the rest of your life are long gone. To be successful in your career and in life, you must frequently be learning new skills and ways of doing things.

The key to life-long learning and becoming an Active Explorer in life is simply having enough confidence in yourself to get out there and get involved. Anytime you initiate involvement in something, you take a risk of failing. However, if you never throw yourself out there, nothing good can happen. Following is a famous quote from Theodore Roosevelt that helps drive this message home. Get out there and actively explore life!

"It is not the critic who counts; nor the man who points out how the strong stumbled, or where the doer of the deed could have done better. The credit belongs to the man who is actually in the arena; whose face is marred by dust and sweat and blood; who strives valiantly; who errs and comes short again and again; who knows the great enthusiasms, the great devotions, and spends himself in a worthy cause; who at the best knows in the end the triumph of high achievements and who at the worst, if he fails, at least fails while daring greatly; so that his place shall never be with those cold and timid souls who know neither victory nor defeat."

—Theodore Roosevelt

THE WHOLE IN ONE

- People make choices based on a limited number of options that they've become exposed to.
- To become an active explorer of life, you must follow the five-step model:
  - **Identify** important criteria of your options.
  - **Read** about your options.
  - **Talk** to people about your options.
  - **Look** at your options.
  - **Experience** your options directly.
- Don't flip a coin to choose your career; go through the same five-step model above when choosing a career.
- Internships and apprenticeships are the best way to "test-drive" careers of interest.
- Take a risk, get out there, and actively explore all that life has to offer!

BECOME THE BEST YOU...BECOME AN ACTIVE EXPLORER!

Chapter 10 Review

Read each question and circle the *best* answer.

1. **Why does the author state that "taking the road less traveled" benefits you?**

   a. You learn a lot about your country.

   b. You learn about other opportunities that may be better for you.

   c. You meet different people.

   d. You get out of your "comfort zone" and become the person you want to be.

2. **There are more than _____ different jobs available within the U.S. economy.**

   a. 20

   b. 220

   c. 2,200

   d. 22,000

3. ***Test-drive* is to *car* as _____ is to *job*.**

   a. internship

   b. school

   c. major

   d. resume

4. **The three (Choosing a Career) steps after (1) identify and (2) read are**

   a. talk, look, experience.

   b. stop, look, listen.

   c. write, talk, interview.

   d. interview, experience, talk.

5. ***Organizing* is to *skill* as _____ is to *interest*.**

   a. speaking

   b. drawing

   c. caring

   d. sports

(continued)

(continued)

6. **When deciding on a career, a good self-assessment would be to assess all of these except**

   a. skills.

   b. interests.

   c. relationships with others.

   d. values.

7. **The best person to ask at a school for self-assessment instruments and exercises is probably a/an**

   a. principal.

   b. English teacher.

   c. physical education teacher.

   d. school counselor.

8. **The acronym POWER in Chapter 10 helps students remember**

   a. how to give an interview.

   b. how to conduct an information interview.

   c. how to write interview answers.

   d. how to pass interviews with flying colors.

9. **Apprenticeship is a way to**

   a. experience careers.

   b. observe careers.

   c. read about careers.

   d. talk about careers.

10. **The best adjective to describe an active explorer is**

    a. hardworking.

    b. adventurous.

    c. resourceful.

    d. loving.

Some Final Thoughts

I hope you enjoyed reading about the 10 Career and Character Education Essentials! Most importantly, I hope you took them to heart and already have begun thinking of ways to incorporate them into your life! Life is way too short to go through the motions and only be a mediocre you. There's nothing worse than looking back over your academic career, your athletic career, your music career, or—most importantly—your life, wondering how good you could have been if you would have given your best. There's no doubt in my mind that if you believe in the 10 Career and Character Education Essentials and work toward making them a part of you, you will *become the best you!*

Remember that the goal is to become the best *you*—not the best *him* or *her* or somebody else. Don't try to be something or somebody that you're not! The *best you* may look very different from that of your friend, brother, sister, or parents. While the 10 Career and Character Education Essentials are important for everybody to develop, you will put your own mark on them.

On that note, I'd like to leave you with a message that was given to me in middle school by one of my role models—a message that has since found its way up on the walls in every one of my bedrooms and offices.

THE MAN IN THE GLASS

When you get what you want in your struggle for self

And the world makes you king for a day,

Just walk to the mirror and take a look at yourself

And see what the man in the glass has to say.

(continued)

(continued)

It isn't your mother, your sweetheart or wife

Whose judgment you must pass,

The fellow whose opinion counts most in your life

Is that man...there...in the glass.

He's the fellow to please, forget all the rest

For he's with you right to the end,

And you'll have passed your most dangerous, most difficult test

If...the man in the glass is your friend.

Sure, you can fool the world as you pass along through the years,

You may even get pats on your back as you pass,

But your only reward will be heartaches and tears,

If you fool...that man in the glass.

—Anonymous

Be true to yourself, give life your best shot, and I know you'll be able to look in the mirror and say, "I have become the best me!"

Top 5 New-Hire Skills and Personal Qualities

A Nine-Year Comparison

Hundreds of recruiters were asked to rate among a long list of skills and qualities they seek in graduates. Following are the top five skills and qualities over the past nine years.

Note the Career and Character Education Essentials that were generated from this first area of research: Become a People Person (Interpersonal Skills); Become a Team Player; Communicate Effectively; Become a Leader (Motivation/Initiative); Become a Person of Integrity (Honesty, Integrity, Work Ethic).

Top Skills and Qualities Employers Look for in Students

2008 Top 5 Skills and Qualities

1. Communication Skills (verbal and written)
2. Strong Work Ethic
3. Teamwork Skills
4. Initiative
5. Interpersonal Skills, Problem-Solving Skills (tied)

2007 Top 5 Skills and Qualities

1. Communication Skills (verbal and written)
2. Honesty/Integrity
3. Interpersonal Skills
4. Motivation/Initiative
5. Strong Work Ethic, Teamwork Skills (tied)

2006 Top 5 Skills and Qualities

1. Honesty/Integrity
2. Communication Skills (verbal and written)
3. Teamwork Skills
4. Strong Work Ethic
5. Interpersonal Skills, Adaptability, Analytical (tied)

2005 Top 5 Skills and Qualities

1. Honesty/Integrity
2. Communication Skills (verbal and written)
3. Interpersonal Skills
4. Strong Work Ethic
5. Teamwork Skills

2004 Top 5 Skills and Qualities

1. Communication Skills (verbal and written)
2. Honesty/Integrity
3. Interpersonal Skills
4. Motivation/Initiative
5. Strong Work Ethic

2003 Top 5 Skills and Qualities

1. Honesty/Integrity
2. Communication Skills (verbal and written)
3. Teamwork Skills
4. Interpersonal Skills
5. Motivation/Initiative

2001 Top 5 Skills and Qualities

1. Communication Skills (verbal and written)
2. Honesty/Integrity
3. Teamwork Skills
4. Interpersonal Skills
5. Motivation/Initiative

2002 Top 5 Skills and Qualities

1. Communication Skills (verbal and written)
2. Honesty/Integrity
3. Teamwork Skills
4. Interpersonal Skills
5. Strong Work Ethic

2000 Top 5 Skills and Qualities

1. Interpersonal Skills
2. Teamwork Skills
3. Verbal Communication
4. Analytical Skills
5. Computer Skills

Source: 2000–2008 NACE Job Outlook Survey, *National Association of Colleges and Employers*

The Increasing Demand for Soft Skills

There is growing evidence that "soft skills" (many of the career and character essentials) are even more important today than they've been in the past.

Note the Career and Character Education Essentials that were generated or reinforced from this second area of research: Become a People Person (interpersonal skills); Become a Team Player; Communicate Effectively; Become a Leader; Become a Person of Integrity (caring, empathy, interpersonal communication); Pay Attention to the Right Things (isolation due to technology).

Personality and Interpersonal Ability Are the Difference Makers

Increasingly, one's personality and interpersonal strengths are the difference makers when it comes to career success and advancement. A study commissioned by the TRACOM Group (Leflein Associates Inc., 2005) surveyed training executives from 100 U.S. companies. Out of the 100 training executives, 94 percent confirmed the importance of interpersonal skills in building and maintaining worker relationships, communicating effectively, managing conflict, and retaining valued employees.

The Shift from IQ to EQ (Emotional Intelligence)

Thanks in great part to the work of Daniel Goleman and his book *Working with Emotional Intelligence* (1998), employers are much more aware of the major impact that soft skills (interpersonal, teamwork, character, integrity, leadership) have on career success. Based on numerous studies that analyze factors influencing job performance, Goleman concludes that emotional competence has a greater impact on job success than IQ does.

Caring, Empathetic Leaders Are Most Successful in Today's Workplace

To become a successful leader or executive today, one must possess a positive, caring personality. In a recent article, "Leadership: Nice guys finish first. Leadership by example" (Citrin, 2006), it appears that the old authoritarian approach to leadership might not be the most effective. Based on research conducted by the executive search firm Spencer Stuart, 90 percent of the top executives reportedly are "unselfish" and "other-oriented," caring greatly about the success of their subordinates. In summary, those who work constructively with others are the ones who advance in their careers and become effective leaders.

The Evolution of Technology and Its Impact on Face-to-Face Interaction

There are so many positive outcomes from technological innovation: increased communication with a wider array of people, enhanced efficiency of workflow and distribution, and e-commerce, to name just a few. Typically, when there is a significant change in lifestyle, you get something new but have to give up something in the process. One of the major concerns with the emergence of our high-tech world is the impact it has on face-to-face interaction, teamwork, and communication—three of the important Career and Character Essentials.

Employers Are Concerned About Graduates' Communication Skills

There appears to be a growing concern among employers regarding the interpersonal and communication ability found in graduates and young employees today, contributing to a further widening of the communication gap. In a 2005 article in the *Pittsburgh Post-Gazette* (online), "Employers Complain About Communication Skills," reporter Jim McKay

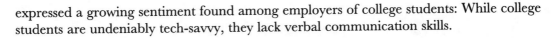

expressed a growing sentiment found among employers of college students: While college students are undeniably tech-savvy, they lack verbal communication skills.

The Internet and Social Isolation

The Internet has had a profound impact on the way we do business and the way that we communicate with each other. However, based on a study conducted at the Stanford Institute for the Quantitative Study of Society (Dixon, 2005), there is strong evidence that the Internet is negatively impacting social interactions. Based on the study, those who use the Internet more frequently spend 70 minutes less daily interacting with family.

Students nowadays are fixated to any number of screens—TVs, computers, e-book readers, iPods, cell phones, and more—making it tough for old-fashioned face-to-face activities and interaction to compete. For each of life's tasks, healthy development depends on ample time spent experiencing or practicing. Just as a baseball player won't improve without batting practice, you won't develop into an effective face-to-face communicator without spending enough time communicating in person with others.

Young people today try to resolve conflicts through text messages, e-mails, and blogs. Looking somebody in the eye and addressing a serious issue is not something you've experienced as frequently as your parents have. When conflicts occur, there is no substitute for sitting down face-to-face with your classmate, friend, or coworker and working things out. It's important to not only listen to what they are trying to say, but also to observe and pick up on their nonverbal cues. Technology is valuable, but in the working world, the most important business is done between real people shaking hands and solving problems together.

Increase of Diversity in the Workplace

The third area of research examined current and future trends in the 21st-century workplace. "Appreciate Diversity" was the main Career and Character Education Essential that emerged from looking at the major trend of "Diversity in the Workplace" as seen below.

Diversity in the Workforce

One of the major trends is the increase of diversity in the workforce. Look at the contrast in diversity from 2005 to the projected diversity in the year 2050.

Ethnic/Racial Percentages in Workforce 2005 (Actual) vs. 2050 (Projection)		
	2005	**2050**
White	74%	61%
Black	10%	12%
Hispanic (may contain members of any race)	12%	20%
Asian and Pacific Islander	4%	7%

Source: Monthly Labor Review, *November 2006, U.S. Department of Labor, Bureau of Labor Statistics*

In addition, the employment rates of women are rising, while those of men are declining somewhat, and an increasing number of persons with disabilities are entering the workforce as well.

The Value of Experience

This fourth area of research centered around attributes and experiences that recruiters valued most in graduates. The Career and Character Education Essentials that emerged were "Become a Leader," "Connect to the World Around You," and "Become an Active Explorer." Recruiters want to see that students have served in a leadership role. They also want students who have been involved in a variety of experiences, including volunteer work, extracurricular activities, and internships. Note that such experience counts almost as much, if not more than, grades.

2008

Employers Rate the Influence of Attributes When Deciding on Two Equally Qualified Candidates

Has held leadership position	4.0
Major	3.9
High GPA (3.0 or above)	3.7
Has been involved in extracurricular activities (clubs, sports, student government, and so on)	3.6
Has done volunteer work	3.0
School attended	2.9

(5-point scale, where 1 = no influence at all; 2 = not much influence; 3 = somewhat of an influence; 4 = very much influence; and 5 = extreme influence)

(continued)

(continued)

Employers' Hiring Preferences Relative to Experience, by Percent of Respondents

I prefer to hire candidates with *relevant* work experience.	76.2%
I prefer to hire candidates with *any type* of work experience (doesn't matter if it's relevant or not, just some type of experience).	18.2%
Work experience doesn't typically factor into my decision when hiring a new college graduate.	4.8%
Other	0.7%

2007

Employers Rate the Influence of Attributes When Deciding on Two Equally Qualified Candidates

Has held leadership position	4.0
Major	4.0
High GPA (3.0 or above)	3.7
Has been involved in extracurricular activities (clubs, sports, student government, and so on)	3.7
Has done volunteer work	3.2
School attended	3.0

(5-point scale, where 1 = no influence at all; 2 = not much influence; 3 = somewhat of an influence; 4 = very much influence; and 5 = extreme influence)

Employer Hiring Preferences Relative to Experience, by Percent of Respondents

I prefer to hire candidates with *relevant* work experience.	74.3%
I prefer to hire candidates with *any type* of work experience (doesn't matter if it is relevant, just some type of experience).	18.9%
Work experience doesn't typically factor into my decision when hiring a new college graduate.	4.2%
Other	2.6%

Source: 2007 NACE Job Outlook Survey *and* 2008 NACE Job Outlook Survey, *National Association of Colleges and Employers*

Using E-portfolios to Reflect on and Market Your Career and Life Experiences

Through reading about the 10 Career and Character Education Essentials, you learned about the experiences that make a difference—internships, leadership in extracurricular activities, and community service, to name a few. Undoubtedly, you will acquire essential skills and qualities through these experiences. However, acquiring skills and being able to identify and articulate those skills are two different things. Many students storm through school and don't take time out to reflect on their experiences and identify the skills and qualities they have acquired.

As you go through school and become active in various groups and activities, it's important to reflect on your experiences so you can identify the skills, qualities, and interests you are developing. You may develop a long list of impressive assets during school, but if you are unable to articulate them effectively to college or company recruiters, you may not do well during interviews.

One of the best new ways to track and market your experiences is to develop an *e-portfolio*. For years, artists have gathered their best works of art and put them into their portfolios to show to potential employers or customers. The same concept applies to e-portfolios. An e-portfolio is a digital or Web document that allows you to gather and organize your experiences and accomplishments, reflect on these experiences, and market yourself to colleges and employers in a multimedia format.

What to Put in Your E-portfolio

Whether you are in middle school or are a high school senior, it is never too early or late to create your own e-portfolio. Here are just some of the items you can gather and present in your e-portfolio:

- As you write those big papers and complete research projects, add them to your e-portfolio.

- After completing a part-time job, internship, or extracurricular activity, write a reflection paper or report for your e-portfolio. Start by summarizing the experience: your essential role or responsibilities, a profile of the organization, and various outcomes or accomplishments. Then reflect on the skills and qualities you developed and what you liked and disliked. If it was an internship or apprenticeship, include a hyperlink to the organization's Web page.

- List the courses you take each year and give a summary of what you learned, what you enjoyed and did not enjoy learning, and any other highlights of the course. Include the name of the teacher and the textbook. You never know who you may want to use as references later.

- Add links to other Web sites that interest you. For example, if you love to hike, create a hiking section in your e-portfolio.

- When it comes time to develop your resume, add an online version of your resume to your portfolio. The added benefit of a Web resume is that it is multidimensional. You can add links from the first page of your resume to second-level pages and so on. For example, you can have the name of the company with which you had the internship (from your internship experience on your resume) be a link to the company's Web site. This enables the recruiter to assess not only what you did during the internship, but also the type of company for which you worked.

- Consider adding samples of your work, whether they are images, videos, excerpts, or any other format. Try to take advantage of the various multimedia capabilities available to you. After all, an e-portfolio should be a dynamic, interesting, and even interactive document.

Sample E-portfolios

One of the best Internet sites for presenting an overview of e-portfolios is Florida State University's Career Portfolio (Figure 1). Following are five figures showing the Career Portfolio system and Information portal presented by the Career Center at Florida State University. Notice how this system enables students to create their own e-portfolios and insert their skills and experiences (Figures 2 and 3) and to ultimately produce their final product (Figure 4). Check out this entire sample online and much more information related to e-portfolios at www.career.fsu.edu/portfolio/ (Figure 5). Click on the "Sample Career Portfolio" link to see an actual example of a career portfolio.

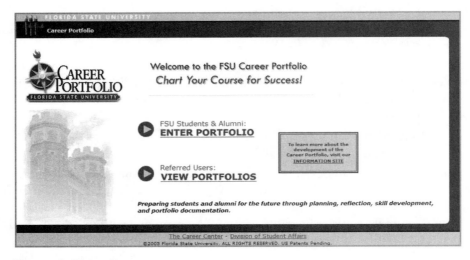

Figure 1: Home Page

Figure 2: Main Menu

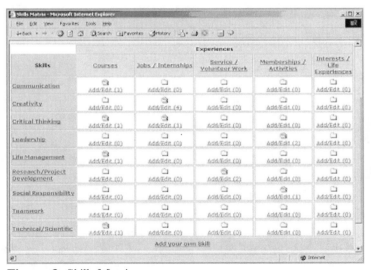

Figure 3: Skills Matrix

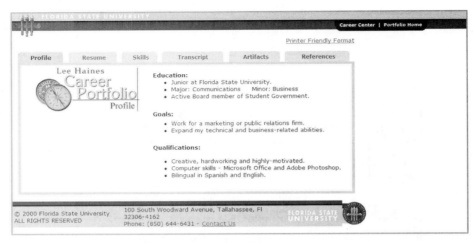

Figure 4: Output of Sample Student's Portfolio

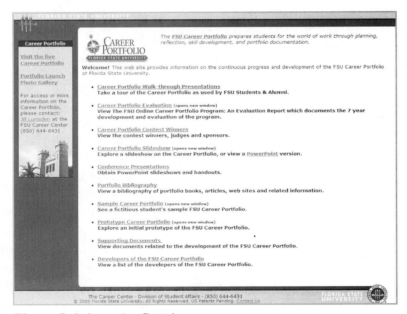

Figure 5: Information Portal

Source: Journal of Career Planning & Employment, *Fall 2001, National Association of Colleges and Employers; Reprinted with permission from NACE and Florida State University authors: Jill A. Lumsden, Jeffrey W. Garis, Robert C. Reardon, Myrna P. Unger, and Scott Arkin.*

Producing Your Own E-portfolio*

Creating the items that you want to include in your e-portfolio is one step in the process; producing your own e-portfolio is another. Talk to your school counselor to see whether your school has any resources that could help you produce your portfolio. Also, look into whether your school provides you with Web space. Many schools now provide their students with space on their Web servers to create their own Web pages. An emerging trend is the use of blogs as e-portfolio spaces.

As you think about what you would add to your portfolio, consider how you will continue to develop it over time. Creating an e-portfolio should not be a one-time event; instead, work to think about what you do in an ongoing way and find ways to reflect on your work at different times.

If you do not have many resources or assistance, here are two easy steps you can take to produce your own e-portfolio using blogging software.

Step One: Develop and Collect Your Portfolio Materials

Identify all the documents, papers, artifacts, images, and links that you want to put in your e-portfolio. Make sure each of your items is of top quality. For example, if you want to include your resume, three term papers, an advertisement you created, a writing sample, and a field study report, you need to make sure each of these items is formatted well, mistake free, and saved on your computer or a disk. Have someone you trust proof your documents.

Think about how each piece could be described in a single blog post and make sure you give each entry a title that describes each piece of work you are highlighting. It also makes a great deal of sense to think about a set of categories to place your entries into. Categories could be as simple as "Term Paper," but using the categories within the blog software will allow you to quickly and easily search for and find the types of work you are looking for.

Step Two: Select Blog Software to Publish Your Portfolio on the Web

There are several free or low-cost options available online. Blogger (www.blogger.com) and Wordpress (www.wordpress.com) are two free, fully featured options. With either of these sites, it is easy to instantly create a personal Web address, set up a customized blog site, and publish text, pictures, video, and links. Both of these services are very easy to use and provide you with a host of excellent tools to design, share, and promote your e-portfolio. For a more involved, career-oriented approach, you can check out www.visualcv.com.

In consultation with Cole W. Camplese—Director of Education Technology Services, Penn State University

Index

R

race-relations courses, 23

reading
about career options, 138–139
improving writing skills, 62

realistic versus dreaming
leadership dynamics, 107

reliability, 70–74

resourcefulness, 77–78

responsibility, personal, 74–78

right thing, doing, 73–74

S

schools
classroom leadership opportunities, 104
improving verbal skills, 63–64
improving writing skills, 61–62
multicultural experiences, 22–24

self-confidence, 44

self-sufficiency, 74–78

sense of humor (interpersonal skills), 9–10

skills
communication skills. See communication skills
interpersonal skills. See interpersonal skills
soft skills, increasing demand for, 152–154
top skills employers look for, 150–151

sleep, dealing with stress, 47

social isolation and Internet, 154

soft skills, increasing demand for, 152–154

stress, rising above, 45–47

studying abroad, 23–24

T

tactfulness (interpersonal skills), 5–6

team players
conflict resolution, 33–36
definition, 30–32
extracurricular activities, 36
impact of technology on, 153–154
interpersonal skills, 32
personal in-group tendencies, 37
volunteering in community, 36

telephone types of communication, 56

tolerating diversity versus appreciating diversity, 17–18

travel
abroad, appreciating diversity, 23–24
connecting to world through, 126–127

U–V

verbal communication
impact of technology on, 154
skills, improving, 63–66
types, 56

video
self-critiquing verbal skills, 65
types of communication, 57

volunteering. *See* community service

W–Z

Web sites
e-portfolios, 160–165
for researching careers, 139

work shadowing, 122, 140

workplace diversity statistics, 155–156

worksheets
Your Attentional Worksheet, 93–94
Your Getting Connected Plan, 127–129

worldly person
community service, 123–125
connecting with the world, 120
public service, 123, 125–126
travel, 126–127
world of work, 120–123
Your Getting Connected Plan worksheet, 127–129

writing
improving, 58–62
types of communication, 57